DR. DAVID E. SMITH is founder and Medical Director of the Haight-Ashbury Free Medical Clinic and Associate Program Director of the West Coast Polydrug Abuse Treatment and Research Project. He is also Assistant Professor of Toxicology at the University of California Medical Center, San Francisco. He is the editor of the *Journal of Psychedelic Drugs*, author of many books and articles, among them the highly acclaimed *The New Social Drug: Cultural, Medical, and Legal Perspectives on Marijuana* (Prentice-Hall, 1970) and *"It's So Good, Don't Even Try It Once": Heroine in Perspective* (Prentice-Hall, 1972). Along with Ben Wooten, Producer, and Ron Wilton, Assistant Producer, and in cooperation with the Haight-Ashbury Free Clinic, he co-produced the film *Glasshouses*, a documentary of case histories of barbiturate and amphetamine abusers.

DR. DONALD R. WESSON was formerly the Chief Psychiatrist at the Haight-Ashbury Free Medical Clinic. He is currently Program Director of the West Coast Polydrug Abuse Treatment and Research Project, and Clinical Instructor in Psychiatry at the University of California, Medical Center, San Francisco.

uppers
and
downers

edited by

David E. Smith, M.D., and Donald R. Wesson, M.D.

Prentice-Hall, Inc. Englewood Cliffs, N. J.

A SPECTRUM BOOK

Library of Congress Cataloging in Publication Data

Smith, David Elvin, 1939–   comp.
    Uppers and downers.

    (A Spectrum Book)
    Includes bibliographies.
    CONTENTS: Smith, D. E. and Wesson, D. R. Introduction:
the politics of uppers and downers.—Kramer, J. C. and Pinco, R. G.
Amphetamine use and misuse: a medicolegal view.—Shick, J. F. E.,
Smith, D. E., and Wesson, D. R. An analysis of amphetamine
toxicity and patterns of use.—Pittel, S. M. and Hofer, R. The
transition to amphetamine abuse.—Eiswirth, N. A., Smith, D. E.,
and Wesson, D. R. Cocaine: champagne of uppers.—Wesson, D. R.
and Smith, D. E. Barbiturate toxicity and the treatment of
barbiturate dependence.—Wesson, D. R., Smith, D. E., and Gay, G. R.
The politics of barbiturate and amphetamine abuse. [etc.]

    1. Drug abuse—Addresses, essays, lectures.
2. Barbiturates—Addresses, essays, lectures.
3. Amphetamine—Addresses, essays, lectures.
I. Wesson, Donald R., joint comp.   II. Title.
[DNLM: 1. Amphetamine. 2. Barbiturates. 3. Drug
abuse. 4. Politics. WM 270 S645u 1973]
HV5801.S566   362.2′9   73–15558
ISBN   0–13–938605–X
ISBN   0–13–938597–5 (pbk.)

DEDICATION

To Sylvia, Alice, Benjamin, Skhy, Santana, and Abra

10 9 8 7 6 5 4 3 2 1

PRENTICE-HALL INTERNATIONAL, INC. (*London*)
PRENTICE-HALL OF AUSTRALIA PTY., LTD. (*Sydney*)
PRENTICE-HALL OF CANADA, LTD. (*Toronto*)
PRENTICE-HALL OF INDIA PRIVATE LIMITED (*New Delhi*)
PRENTICE-HALL OF JAPAN, INC. (*Tokyo*)

ACKNOWLEDGMENTS

The editors express their appreciation to the *Journal of Psychedelic Drugs* for help in preparing this book. The following chapters have appeared in slightly modified form in the *Journal of Psychedelic Drugs*, Volume 5, Issue 2, Winter, 1972. Amphetamine Use and Misuse: A Medicolegal View, An Analysis of Amphetamine Toxicity and Patterns of Use, Barbiturate Toxicity and the Treatment of Barbiturate Dependence, Legitimate and Illegitimate Distribution of Amphetamines and Barbiturates, Methaqualone: Just Another Downer, and Cocaine: Champagne of Uppers. The Corporate Pushers is reprinted from *Playboy*, September, 1972. The Ethics of Addiction is reprinted from the *American Journal of Psychiatry*, November, 1971.

We express our appreciation to the current and former staff of Donald R. Wesson Associates: to Anne Gilhool, who typed numerous drafts; to Nancy Eiswirth, who assisted with data collection and research; to Laurie Linda, for typing and editorial assistance; and to Ben Wooten and Ron Wilton, who co-produced with Dr. Smith *Glasshouses,* a film on uppers and downers, for his help in our field research particularly in the areas of "straight" amphetamine and barbiturate abuse. *Glasshouses* is distributed by Haight-Ashbury Films, 701 Irving Street, San Francisco, California 94122, and by See Saw films, P.O. Box 262, Palo Alto, California 94302.

CONTENTS

introduction:
the politics
of uppers and downers

David E. Smith, M.D. /
Donald R. Wesson, M.D.

Most people are aware that during the past decade drug abuse has become a highly sensitive political issue. Few realize, however, the extent to which divergent political factors influence the nation's scattered and often misdirected efforts at coping with drug abuse problems. This book attempts to make the reader aware of one major and relatively unknown aspect of the drug problem—the abuse of stimulants and depressants. We have compiled a selection of diverse and even conflicting views which we hope will serve to stimulate dialogue and further consideration of problems involving uppers and downers.

Government agencies vary in their degrees of expertise in drug-abuse issues and it is easy to fault a particular group for shortsightedness or bureaucratic incompetence. The daily newspaper gives many examples of poorly designed, inefficient government programs, and naive statements by public officials concerning drug abuse. Nor are government agencies beyond intentionally falsifying—or selectively releasing—information for their own benefit. Legislation designed to regulate and control illegal traffic in drugs often is perverted to enhance the bureaucratic self-esteem of another agency or to bring oppressive forces against political and racial minorities, or against that minority group labeled "the mentally ill."

Health care delivery systems are deeply influenced by the prevailing political climate. In spite of the currently popular "enlightened" view that drug abuse is primarily a medical-social problem, most of the programs directed toward solving the nation's drug problem are devised on bureaucrätic levels with minimal input from the communities at risk. Medical and community concerns now, as always, take a back seat to political and legal issues in dealing with drug abuse. The evolution of laws relating to the treatment of opium addicts illustrates this point dramatically; however, these discrepancies have been carefully documented in other books.

For a variety of reasons the abuse of uppers and downers is subject even more than opiate abuse to political advantage-seeking. Although widespread social concern over uppers and downers has developed much more recently than concern over the opiates such as heroin, we believe the same mistakes will be made in dealing with their regulation unless enough individuals knowledgeable in the past politics of opiate abuse intervene. Our observations support the view that the true nature of the political and medical-social interface is still largely unrecognized by the individuals who need to be most aware of this interface—drug program administrators and drug abusers.

We have chosen to focus on the politics of uppers and downers for several reasons. During 1971, we testified at Senate subcommittee hearings concerning the abuse of amphetamines and barbiturates. This experience heightened our sensitivity to many political and economic facets of these drugs, and gave us access to vast quantities of data from all parts of the country concerning the abuse of those psychoactive chemicals.

In addition, we are concerned that today both national policy and public attention are focused almost entirely upon heroin and, to a lesser extent, marijuana. Data collected in several parts of the country indicate that the incidence of *new* heroin addicts is declining, while nonmedical use of stimulants—especially cocaine—and downers—especially barbiturates and methaqualone—is rapidly increasing. Further drug use and abuse is shifting toward multiple or polydrug abuse. While not wishing to minimize the severity or extent of the heroin problem in the U.S., we believe that much of what currently passes as medically indicated treatment for heroin addiction has as its underlying motivation economic, legal, political, and social control goals.

Abuse of uppers and downers produces a cluster of economic, political, medical, and public-health problems which differ considerably from the problems of heroin abuse. The direct cost of preventive drug-control measures and arrest statistics is irrelevant to the pharmacological properties of the drugs, although it reflects the vigor with which the related drug laws are enforced. The cost of the drug to the consumer, however, is a major determinant in the life style which develops around the use of the drug. Whereas a heroin habit is expensive ($25 to $100 per day), a stimulant or barbiturate habit costs only a few dollars per day to maintain.

This high consumer cost factor produces most of the visible everyday realities of the heroin addict's life style—the usual reliance on illegal fund raising, and the endless varieties of "junkie" games. Since the new-style junkie is literally "at home" in middle- and upper-income communities, he plays his games there, producing a direct and annoying economic impact on the community in the form of increased homeowners' and auto-theft insurance, missing TVs, etc.

Neither the "speed freaks" nor the "barb freaks" consistently resort to such crimes against property on a daily basis, since they can support their habit from regular employment, panhandling, welfare checks, or other less irritating fund raising techniques. In many cases, this lack of organized criminal activity may not be voluntary. The speed freak simply may be too paranoid and unreliable for the organized criminal world while the stoned barb freak is likely to wreck the getaway car.

Cocaine, a potent stimulant or upper, has returned after decades of relatively little use as a new fad. From a public-threat standpoint, cocaine combines the drug toxicity of "speed" with the economic problems of heroin. As witnessed by recent highly publicized "cocaine scandals" in the National Football League and Columbia Broadcasting System, this potent stimulant has penetrated the middle and upper classes of American society.

Related to the economic issue is the source of supply. While everyone is aware that heroin traffic involves organized criminal activity, the primary sources of stimulants and barbiturates are prominent pharmaceutical companies many of whom are listed on the New York Stock Exchange. While we must not overlook the fact that the pharmaceutical industry produces many drugs of unquestionable value in the practice of medicine, one wonders to what extent the economic influence of the industry—including the lobbying efforts of the Pharmaceutical Manufacturers' Association—has hindered the development of rational controls over the supply of uppers and downers.

There is now federal and public awareness that large numbers of American troops have experimented with—or become addicted to —heroin while in Vietnam. This has, of course, been a source of annoyance and embarrassment to the Nixon Administration. The effort to continue support of Thieu's regime in South Vietnam was a major political factor influencing the appropriation of money into "crash programs" for the development of long-acting narcotic antagonists which could "immunize" troops against the possibility of heroin addiction. It must be emphasized that these measures were aimed only at opiate abuse and do not touch the massive amphetamine, barbiturate, or alcohol problem in the military.

We would like to underscore that we are not opposed to spending for either research into or treatment of heroin addiction. Rather, our criticism is directed toward the politically motivated funneling of virtually all drug-treatment and research resources into heroin-related problems. We perceive that the primary motivation for this one-sided allocation of funds is to achieve reduction in crime rates and protection of a political image. While crime reduction is certainly a worthwhile goal, it should be approached openly, and not under the pretext of supplying "medical treatment" for drug abusers. Our irritation over this issue becomes acute each time we try to arrange treatment for a barbiturate or amphetamine abuser and are faced with the extreme inadequacy of existing programs and facilities.

Five to ten million individuals in this country are estimated to use amphetamines or barbiturates without medical supervision. For example, "exposés" have demonstrated the widespread use of stimulants in highly competitive college and professional sports. Lord Lambton, Finance Minister of England, resigned recently after being caught in his London townhouse with amphetamines and other drugs which he used with a variety of high class prostitutes to heighten sexual experience. But to what extent does such varied drug use represent a problem?

Certainly the incidence of use, alone, of a particular drug cannot be equated with the severity of a national drug problem and we would not like to compound past errors by indicating that amphetamines and barbiturates create larger drug problems than heroin simply because more individuals use amphetamines and barbiturates than heroin.

By the same token, social or medical toxicity of a drug cannot, by itself, define the severity of the problem. Intravenous barbiturate use, for example, has both high morbidity and high mortality, but this intravenous pattern of drug use still involves relatively few individuals. Rational assessment of the severity of a drug abuse problem must consider *both* the incidence of use and the toxicity of the drug in order to determine the overall effect of that drug pattern on society as a whole.

Furthermore, it is pointless to argue over which drug is the biggest problem. Each drug produces its own set of problems—which may not be directly comparable to others. Robberies, for example, are more likely to be associated with heroin addiction; auto accidents are more apt to be associated with barbiturate or alcohol abuse; and unprovoked violence with abuse of amphetamines. What uniform comparisons can be made among these phenomena?

Focus upon national economic or crime-control criteria, rather than humanistic or medical concerns, to establish priorities for drug treatment programs has for several years financially hampered the development of a "barbiturate antagonist" which could reverse the respiratory depression and cardiovascular toxicity of barbiturate overdose. The pharmaceutical industry has been less than enthusiastic about developing such a compound without government support because of its "limited market value." For example, a pharmaceutical company had in the animal-testing stage a barbiturate compound antagonist which appeared promising; however, since the company was aiming to design an antidepressant with wide market appeal it was not interested in developing the compound as a limited-use barbiturate antagonist.

This illustrates the current political-economic dilemma of new drug development. The high cost of bringing a new drug from the animal laboratory testing stage to approval by the Food and Drug Administration for nonexperimental medical use means that a "limited-use" item—regardless of the medical need—cannot be expected to provide a profitable return. Within a profit-making framework, the anticipated market must be sufficient to offset both development and marketing costs. Thus, the last few years have seen the market flooded with a proliferation of "me too" drugs because these repetitious drugs bring in the most income for the producer—designed for the treatment of chronic, common conditions such as insomnia, depression, and anxiety—that only contribute to our country's obsessive drug orientation.

The chapters that follow contain many differing and even contradictory opinions concerning social-political facets of uppers and downers, as well as the broader aspects of drug abuse in American society.

The chapter on "The Legitimate and Illegitimate Distribution of Amphetamines and Barbiturates" summarizes our views on how legitimately manufactured drugs find their way to the street. We emphasize the importance of gaining an overall perspective on the picture of drug diversion; otherwise, piecemeal controls will only result in diversion being switched from one channel to another.

Admittedly our own recommendations are very much oriented toward control of the supply of amphetamines and barbiturates. We emphasize "supply" because we have seen too many examples of laws intended to prevent drug abuse being selectively enforced or perverted for political reasons when they are applied only to the user or at the "street" level.

The impact on the availability and price of uppers and downers on the drug black market must be monitored as the supply of legitimately manufactured uppers and downers decreases. While it is unlikely that the demand is sufficiently strong to create a black market situation comparable to that which exists for heroin, it would be most unfortunate to recreate with uppers and downers the conditions which have led to the development of the "criminal" heroin addict.

As the available usable supply of these drugs is reduced, easily accessible treatment facilities must be available to addicts who wish to be cured of their habit. The problem does not cease with the treatment of physical dependence. Comprehensive health services must be available to treat the frequently underlying medical or psychological difficulties which the addict was "self-medicating" with stimulants or depressants.

We view controls aimed at drug companies as necessary stopgap measures which can have as their best result the disengaging of legitimate drug companies from the "pusher" role. Further, we believe that physicians prescribing amphetamines and barbiturates must become better trained and better informed about the complexities of the drug scene in order to stop being, in effect, "middlemen drug dealers" for legitimately manufactured psychoactive drugs.

By emphasizing responsible drug-taking behavior, demand for these agents will be reduced, but it is inconceivable to us that there will ever be a time when no drugs are abused for there will always be individuals who use drugs in a way which is detrimental to themselves or hazardous to other members of society.

Andrew Weil in his book, *The Natural Mind,* proposes that the altering of one's state of consciousness is an innate human drive, and points out that the use of drugs as one means of producing altered states of consciousness has been a feature of human life in all places on the earth and in all ages of history—with the exception of the Eskimos.

At some point we must begin to distinguish between efforts whose effect is merely to limit individual freedom of choice of chemicals for altering consciousness, and those designed to protect society against the irresponsible activities of those individuals who use drugs in such a way as to create a danger to others.

The widespread drug-use phenomenon which has emerged within the past ten years, however, cannot be discounted as solely the activity of misfits, psychopaths, or "crazies." As a mass phenomenon, widespread drug abuse reflects the inability of substantial numbers and subgroups within our society to find a purpose or meaning in existence beyond the temporary solace found in drugs. That this phenomenon has occurred in a drug-oriented society which actively supports such pharmacological solutions though a cradle-to-grave message of "better living through chemistry" and "a pill for all ills" is hardly coincidental.

amphetamine use and misuse:
a medico-legal view

John C. Kramer, M.D. / Robert G. Pinco, Esq.

introduction

A muscular but glum mountaineer stares distantly out of an advertising page of a psychiatric journal. It's 10:25 and he's still home. Copy on the facing page suggests that the advertised stimulant may help get him over the hump. It promises that "as increased enthusiasm and vigor replace tiredness, new projects get started."

The advertisement is unfortunate. It emphasizes one of the most questionable uses of stimulants; that is, to provide a feeling of well-being and energy to otherwise physically healthy individuals. By warning, in small print at the bottom of the facing page, that this drug should not be used to increase mental or physical capacities beyond physiological limits, the manufacturer fulfilled FDA requirements while directly contradicting his principal message. It would be far better for this melancholic mountaineer to remain at home than to jeopardize himself and his fellows while high both in the mountains and on the stimulant. The thrust of the particular advertising campaign has been largely toward the use of this stimulant for fatigue and mild depression rather than toward other uses, which though offering a smaller market are less questionable medically. Since that advertisement appeared, the FDA has asked advertisers to refrain from suggesting that psychoactive drugs be prescribed to allay the ordinary discomforts and anxieties of everyday life.

The euphoriant effect of amphetamines (and related compounds) is responsible for their popularity among patients, an event which in turn induced excessive prescribing by physicians. The use of these stimulants is accompanied by tolerance to their effects which often leads to the need for increasing quantities in order to produce a sustained effect. In addition, even those who use clinically prescribed quantities for an extended period find that discontinuation produces lethargy and a sense of need to persist in its use, in other words, dependence. Thus, people continue the use of stimulants not merely because it makes them feel good, but also because withdrawal produces unpleasant effects. The withdrawal symptoms, though not as dangerous or painful as those which accompany discontinuation of opiates or sedative-hypnotics, are in fact entirely analogous. While withdrawal from opiates or barbiturates produces a rebound over-stimulation, withdrawal from amphetamines produces a rebound physiological depression characterized by fatigue and lethargy.

Unquestionably, a large proportion of prescriptions for amphetamines, though nominally intended for appetite suppression or for relief of mild chronic fatigue, are actually used for satisfying the craving for euphoria and to stave off the depression which follows withdrawal. Amphetamine-seeking patients frequently practice deception on their physicians and on themselves. Some patients ask for the amphetamine for presumed medical purposes, fully aware that their real intention is to use it as a euphoriant, while others deceive even themselves with their own rationalizations.

marketing amphetamines

The 1970 *Physicians' Desk Reference (PDR)*, a compilation of information on the most commonly prescribed drugs, listed about 50 different trade names of stimulants in the amphetamine group. Appetite control was by far the predominant indication for their use, and in some instances the only one. The second most prominent suggested indication was for symptomatic relief of mild depressive states. Only a few preparations listed were proposed for use in the treatment of hyperactive children or narcolepsy, the only undisputed indications. That is pretty much the story of the marketing of the stimulants. Only a small, though growing proportion of the prescribing is for purposes which can be considered fully warranted.

Some products have contained amphetamines in addition to vitamins, hormones, or other medications. In some instances, it appears that the manufacturers' intent is to offer vitamin supplements to dieters; in others the intent is to offer the product primarily as a nutritional supplement while the purpose of the added amphetamine would appear to be to provide the patient a sense of well being which he will attribute to the dietary supplement but which will, in fact, be due to the stimulant.

Thus, most of the manufacturers can be faulted for exploiting the most questionable uses of amphetamines, namely, appetite suppression, relief of mild depression, and relief of fatigue. In a few instances, manufacturers' descriptions and advice in the *PDR* could have lead to serious errors in the patient management. In 1970 three manufacturers described maximum doses of amphetamines in excess of 50 milligrams per day, a dosage which if used persistently, might produce psychotic states (Connell 1958). Other instances of poor judgment in manufacturers' descriptions in the *PDR* have included recommendations for evening as well as morning use, though evening use is contraindicated because of the insomnia which may be produced; statements suggesting that dependence is not a problem; and recommendations for use in the treatment of alcoholics, a group notoriously prone to misuse any psychoactive drug. The 1973 edition of *PDR* still presents appetite control as the predominant indication for the amphetamines, but has corrected the most glaring defects.

In his review of the use of amphetamines in obesity, Penick (1969) concludes that amphetamine over a short period of time will produce weight loss, but he indicates that this effect dissipates after four to eight weeks. He also brings into clear focus differences of opinion between psychiatrists on one hand and internists, general practitioners and obstetricians on the other, the former recommending drastic reductions in prescribing, the latter group viewing amphetamines as useful and with relatively few complications. Penick says:

> Psychiatrists see the complications of amphetamine usage: they see toxic psychoses, psychological habituation, etc. But those of us who use these drugs to treat obesity have many patients who have tolerated them well over a period of years without overusing them or becoming habituated. There is no question that overuse and habituation are problems; however, there is no way of accurately estimating the statistical risk involved in prescribing an amphetamine for an obese patient (1969).

Still, he suggests limiting the use of stimulants for dietary control to the following: Early in the weight reduction program of obese patients; intermittently to suppress occasional overwhelming hunger; and for the slightly overweight patient with a limited goal of weight reduction.

Amphetamines are of even more doubtful value as a treatment for "mild depression" (Wheatley 1969). The euphoria which they produce is short lived and the sense of depression which follows as the drug effect wears off is frequently deeper than that for which the drug was prescribed. Included in the rubric of "mild depression" may be a state characterized by a sense of lack of energy or ambition. It would appear that there are many patients who take moderate quantities of amphetamines daily without apparent difficulty, who when they discontinue its use find themselves lethargic and unable to function as they think they should. Some, of course, ultimately increase their regular dose and experience toxic effects. No information exists as to what proportion of this group of patients go on to use excessive doses. Regular use of even moderate quantities of amphetamines may result in lethargy when the patient stops using it.

recognized medical uses

In general, then, amphetamines tend to be ineffective in depression, and may even make it worse, though one special case should be noted. Use of combinations of tricyclic antidepressants or monamine oxidase inhibitor antidepressants with amphetamines has been effective in some instances of otherwise intractable depression. Because this combination carries a serious risk of acute hypertension, it is experimental only and should not be employed without great care and informed consent of the patient.

The value of amphetamines in the treatment of some hyperactive children was initially reported in 1937 (Bradley) and has been reviewed by Cole (1969). Some children who demonstrate a pattern of hyperactivity and excessively short attention span may be destructive, belligerent and generally exasperating. Many, though not all of such children are paradoxically slowed down by stimulants so that their ability to learn improves and they become acceptable not only to their parents and teachers but equally to their siblings, their classmates and themselves. Though some politicians and reporters (von Hoffman 1970) have suggested that this use of amphetamines was tantamount to thought control, such statements are grossly irresponsible. They depict these children as bright, seeking and impatient, bored by dull teachers who merely want to subjugate them. In fact, the children seem driven to persistent disruptive behavior which is beyond their capacity to control and is not much affected by even the most patient, understanding or imaginative parents or teachers. In such children amphetamines often reduce their driven and destructive activity to a level consistent with other children without creating excessive passivity. The possibility of toxicity or dependence has been of concern but fortunately no such instance has been reported and generally the medication is discontinued in early adolescence though some patients may need treatment through their mid-teens. As with any medication or treatment, it can, in overenthusiastic hands, be misapplied.

Narcolepsy is an uncommon disease characterized by an intermittent, irresistible need to sleep which tends to occur most often under conditions which even in nonnarcoleptics would tend to produce drowsiness. It is the irresistible quality of this need for sleep and its repetitive occurrence which defines the disease. Though the patient usually wakens after a brief sleep, the disorder is annoying and disruptive. Amphetamines are highly effective in its treatment, and though some sufferers need fairly large doses, generally once an adequate daily dose is found, it can be continued without increase and without danger for many years.

Following recovery from some forms of viral encephalitis, brain damage may bring about a form of Parkinson's disease which besides rigidity and tremor, may be accompanied by persistent excessive drowsiness. This symptom generally yields to treatment with amphetamines and as in the treatment of narcolepsy, once a suitable dose is found, increase is seldom found necessary. Oculogyric crises, paroxysmal movements of the eyes, which may also accompany it may also be helped by treatment with amphetamines.

Other acceptable uses for amphetamines include combating drowsiness produced by other medications; as an aid to exploratory psychotherapy; and on rare occasions, in serious emergencies when continued functioning is necessary despite extreme fatigue.

misuse of amphetamines

Speculation started regarding Benzedrine's potential for abuse shortly after its introduction (Peoples and Guttman 1936) and careless use for nonmedical purposes was noted as early as 1937 (*JAMA*). During the next 20 years, a few instances of toxicity with paranoid states were noted, as were instances of abuse, but experience suggested that both abuse and toxicity were infrequent compared to the extensive use of this drug. As recently as 1957 (Leake), the paranoid state which was occasionally seen in some users was thought to

occur only in those who suffered from a latent underlying schizophrenia, and generally into the early 1960s, amphetamine dependence, whatever its theoretical likelihood, was not considered of great
practical significance. The methamphetamine epidemic which had
occurred in Japan during the late 1940s and early 1950s (Brill and
Hirose 1969), had not been widely publicized in the United States,
and until the mid-1960s, little attention had been focused on the
growing problem here.

Recently, abuse of amphetamines by adolescents and young adults,
either in a pattern of occasional sprees or of persistent high-dose use
has drawn most attention; abuse by adults who obtain their supplies
legally is both less dramatic and more difficult to discover but may,
in fact, be more extensive. It seems probable that in most instances,
this adult form of abuse is characterized by a false sense of therapeutic need for the drug and a feeling of incapacity, fatigue, and
depression when the drug is not used contrary to the adolescent and
young adult abuse pattern in which pleasure is the primary objective. In some instances of the adult pattern, toxic symptoms may be
present and are characterized mainly by irritability and insomnia.
Occasionally, paranoid symptoms appear which are rarely correctly
diagnosed as due to amphetamine use. The incidence of this pattern
of amphetamine abuse should be reduced as physicians become more
cautious about prescribing amphetamines for fatigue, mild depression and weight reduction, the conditions for which most amphetamines are dispensed. Were prescriptions for weight loss and fatigue
eliminated, the total legal demand would decrease considerably and
simplify the problems of policing the distribution of the remainder
of the supplies.

A substantial decrease in legitimate though unwarranted prescribing would decrease the total supply available for diversion to the
illegal market. Under these circumstances, it is possible that illicit
chemical synthesis would partially replace the supplies lost by the
reduction in legitimate amphetamines available for diversion.
Though there would probably be an important reduction in adult
abusive use, there would be a lesser reduction among high-dose users
and others who rely primarily on illicit channels. Methamphetamine
in particular is not difficult to prepare, requiring simple chemical
equipment and two reagents, one easily obtained and one which is
obtained with somewhat greater difficulty. Nevertheless, there seems
little to be lost and much to be gained by substantially diminishing
the use and production of amphetamines for medical purposes.

It has been stated that during the 1960s one third to one half of the legally produced amphetamines in the United States ultimately ended in illicit channels. As a measure of magnitude of production, the 100,000 pounds of amphetamines produced in 1962 would have supplied about 8 billion therapeutic doses. Until mid-1970, one of the techniques for diversion from legitimate supplies entailed the ordering of drugs in immense lots by pharmacies (real or fictitious) in Mexico. The amphetamines (and barbiturates) were brought legally into Mexico and distributed there or were picked up from warehouses in the United States and disappeared without crossing the border. Other means of diversion include direct thefts from warehouses and pharmacies, falsifying inventories, and fraudulent orders by people representing themselves as physicians or researchers (Durrin 1970).

Some unethical physicians may add large quantities of amphetamines to the market. The "patient" visits the physician with the intention of obtaining amphetamines (and often barbiturates as well). He may be quite direct in his request, though usually he will present some spurious medical indication for the drug. The doctor may then write a prescription or dispense a supply from an office stock. The physician may measure the "patient's" blood pressure and take his pulse. This cursory examination fulfills the basic legal requirements that the physician examine the patient prior to prescribing for him. Other physicians who specialize in the treatment of obesity dispense and prescribe prodigious quantities of amphetamines. Though claiming to use proper care in prescribing, their ethics if not their legality can be questioned.

Though some physicians practice in the ethical borderlands of medicine, there are still some well within the mainstream of the profession who view the use of amphetamines for the treatment of mild depression and for weight reduction as effective and safe. Serious toxic reaction is uncommon and easily controlled in their opinion and dependence is a rare phenomenon. It is from this body of medical opinion that the pharmaceutical manufacturers and distributors gained their strongest argument for producing a large volume of stimulants. The drug companies are there, after all, to supply those accepted pharmaceutical agents which ethical physicians in their professional judgments believe are necessary for their patients. A physician is free not to prescribe amphetamines if he feels they are dangerous, but, goes the manufacturer's argument, those doctors who believe amphetamines to be useful and relatively safe under medical supervision should not be prohibited from prescribing them.

Public concern over abuse of psychoactive drugs sometimes centers on its presumed tendency to induce unwarranted violence. Heroin and other opiates do not directly cause violence. Though a heroin user could, for instance, commit an act of violence during a robbery, there is nothing in the drug effect which would so incline him. Heroin is more likely to inhibit any tendency toward violent behavior.

On the other hand amphetamines do tend to set up conditions in which violent behavior will occur (Ellinwood 1971). Suspiciousness and hyperactivity produced by large doses of amphetamines may combine to induce precipitous and unwarranted assaultive behavior. Under their influence, lability of mood is common, the user abruptly shifting from warmly congenial to furiously hostile moods for the most trivial reasons. This lability of affect can be seen in Andy Warhol's cinema verité film, *The Chelsea Girls,* in which a character called "The Pope" injects himself with speed and then takes the role of confessor to a young woman. At first effusively benevolent, he becomes angry and assaultive when he accuses her of failing to participate in her role with sufficient enthusiasm. He drags her off the set and then returns on camera. Gradually, his temper cools and he expresses his forgiveness of her. The whole scene rings so true, one may reasonably suspect that real amphetamine was used.

Most high dose amphetamine users describe involvement, either as aggressor or victim, in episodes in which murder or mayhem was avoided by the slimmest of margins. There are, of course, instances in which violence actually occurred. From descriptions of a number of these events it seems probable that they would not have occurred had it not been for the use of amphetamines. Within certain dosage ranges of amphetamines, caged mice, ordinarily peaceful animals, regularly slaughter one another.

The role of barbiturates in this is difficult to assess. It is regularly reported by many drug users that when barbiturate use is not followed by sleep it often induces considerable irritability (though opiates, cannabis and the phenothiazines tend to be calming). Users of amphetamines often use barbiturates for sedation and this may add to, rather than diminish, a tendency toward angry or violent behavior.

controls over medical use

The major moves to legislatively restrict amphetamine distribution beyond the sale by prescription only (required in the Federal Food,

Drug and Cosmetic Act) began in the early sixties. Diversion of amphetamines had reached alarming proportions. Public pressure was mounting to control these drugs in much the same way as morphine and other opiates had been controlled under the Federal narcotics laws. President Kennedy appointed Judge E. Barrett Prettyman as Chairman of the President's Advisory Commission on Narcotics and Drug Abuse in early 1963, and that Commission recommended new Federal legislation to control amphetamines (U.S. Congress 1970).

Finally, in early 1965 the 89th Congress considered and then adopted H.R. 2, the Drug Abuse Control Amendments to the Federal Food, Drug and Cosmetic Act. Both the House Interstate and Foreign Commerce Committee and the Senate Labor and Public Welfare Committee studied H.R. 2 and attributed the need for such legislation to the "sieve-like" distribution system of amphetamines in the United States (U.S. Congress 1965). Both Committees stated that the U.S. drug distribution system had caused massive diversion of amphetamines out of the legitimate channels of distribution into the black market. The Committees estimated that almost 50% of the over 9 billion dosage units of amphetamines (and barbiturates) produced annually had been diverted into the black market. They attributed the general availability of amphetamines on the black market to little or no self-regulation of distribution by pharmaceutical manufacturers and wholesalers and to overprescribing by physicians (U.S. Congress 1965).

Though developing a strong case for very stringent control of amphetamines, both committees opted for lesser controls. They rejected controls similar to those placed upon narcotics by stating "one approach which the Committee considered is the approach used in the laws relating to hard narcotics under which extremely rigid controls are placed on raw materials, and upon manufacture and distribution of narcotics. . . . The Committee felt that the imposition of rigid controls of this type is not warranted at the present time, at least until the milder form of regulation constrained in this legislation has been tried" (U.S. Congress 1965).

Instead, the controls designed by the House Committee were basically record keeping rules for manufacturers, wholesalers and pharmacies. The bulk of the physicians who prescribed or dispensed amphetamines were exempted from registration and from the record-keeping requirements of the Drug Abuse Control Amendments. The only restrictions were upon the number of times a physician could authorize a prescription to be refilled, i.e. up to five times in a six month period. However, no limits were placed on the quantity of

medication which could be prescribed, nor were government order
forms required for distribution of these drugs. The lack of controls
over manufacture and exportation, and the lack of registration of
physicians and pharmacies severely restricted enforcement by the
Bureau of Drug Abuse Control which was then part of the Food
and Drug Administration. Little could be done about overproduc-
tion and diversion from legitimate channels of distribution. The
Bureau of Drug Abuse Control was unable to pinpoint specific
points of diversion. In addition, large quantities of amphetamines
continued to be produced by certain U.S. drug manufacturers, exported without controls, repackaged and smuggled back into this
country by clandestine methods.

The Drug Abuse Control Amendments of 1965 were largely ineffective in either decreasing diversion out of legitimate channels of
distribution, or in significantly decreasing overprescribing by physicians.

In 1968, the Bureau of Drug Abuse Control under the Food and
Drug Administration was merged with the Federal Bureau of Narcotics then under the Treasury Department. The new agency, the
Bureau of Narcotics and Dangerous Drugs (BNDD) was placed in
the Department of Justice (Presidential Reorganization Plan 1968).
The following year a comprehensive revision of all the narcotic and
dangerous drug laws was sent to Congress immediately following a
ten-point Presidential message calling for an all out effort to curb
drug abuse in the United States (U.S. Congress 1969). Some eighteen
months later Public Law 91–513 emerged as the Comprehensive
Drug Abuse Prevention and Control Act of 1970 (known popularly
as the Controlled Substances Act) (U.S. Code 1973). This new law
repealed all of the previous laws, including the Drug Abuse Control
Amendments of 1965, and set up a five-schedule system for controlling all abusable substances. Amphetamines, methamphetamine,
and most of the amphetamine-like drugs were placed in schedule III,
with the exception of methamphetamine in liquid injectable form
which was placed in schedule II.

Schedule III of the new Controlled Substances Act paralleled the
controls of the Drug Abuse Control Amendments of 1965 by placing
a limit on authorization of prescription refills and a limit of 6
months on the life of a prescription. The controls in schedule II
which were extremely strict were analogous to the former controls
over class "A" and "B" narcotics under the repealed Harrison Narcotic Act. Schedule II controls required written prescriptions, quotas
on total production and special government order forms for distri-

bution of substances from the pharmaceutical manufacturer through the wholesaler to the pharmacy or physician. Import and export restrictions, as well as special security controls, were also included.

On May 30, 1971, the Controlled Substances Act became effective. Approximately one month later BNDD proposed administrative rescheduling of all amphetamines and methamphetamine (Federal Register 1971; Baumgartner and Morrell 1972). The proposed regulation used a concept successfully developed under the 1965 Drug Abuse Control Amendments (DACA). The DACA concept had provided for administrative action by the Federal Government (as opposed to new legislation) to place central nervous system stimulants or depressants under control if they met certain abuse criteria (U.S. Congress 1973).

The concept was expanded in the new Controlled Substances Act to include administrative scheduling and rescheduling of any abusable substances based upon such factors as the drug's actual or relative potential abuse; scientific evidence of that drug's pharmacological effect, if known; the state of current scientific knowledge regarding the drug or other substance; the drug's history and current pattern of abuse; what, if any, risks there were to the public health; and the psychic or physiological dependence liability of that drug (U.S. Code 1973).

In addition to the general factors, each schedule had its own special criteria. In order to move a drug from schedule III to schedule II of the Controlled Substances Act, the BNDD was required to show that amphetamines and methamphetamine had a high potential for abuse, that these drugs had some currently accepted medical use with severe restrictions, and that their abuse could lead to severe psychological or physical dependence (U.S. Code 1973).

Believing that amphetamine or methamphetamine should have been placed in schedule II in the original legislation, BNDD devoted much effort from the signing of the Act into law by President Nixon on October 27, 1970, until its effective date, May 30, 1971, gathering evidence for what it believed would be a major battle with the U.S. drug manufacturers. The battle never materialized and, in fact, virtually all of these drugs were controlled by mid-July, 1971, less than two months after the Controlled Substances Act became effective. The thrust of the movement of amphetamines, methamphetamine, and certain amphetamine combination products to schedule II was to place the severe schedule II restrictions discussed above upon these substances.

In early 1972, the Federal Bureau of Narcotics and Dangerous

Drugs set production quotas for amphetamines and methamphetamine at approximately 22% of the 1971 production figures. Their action was taken in light of a statement of concern by the Surgeon General and because of the August 8, 1970, Food and Drug Administration modified labeling requirements for amphetamines (Federal Register 1972). The FDA labeling requirement had limited prescribing of amphetamines to three medical indications: narcolepsy, hyperkinetic disorders of children, and short-term obesity control. In the spring of 1973 the Food and Drug Administration withdrew their New Drug Application (NDA) approval for injectable amphetamine and methamphetamine, as well as, for combination anorexients (Federal Register 1973). The FDA found that these injectable and combination products were no longer safe and effective for any medical use and should be withdrawn from the market. In response to this action, the Federal Bureau of Narcotics and Dangerous Drugs on May 8, 1973 again slashed quotas for production of amphetamine and methamphetamine to approximately 11% of the 1971 production figures. In essence, approximately a 90% production decrease was effected within two years after passage of the Controlled Substances Act.

The moderate restrictions placed on practitioners in the mid-sixties had proven ineffective in reducing or eliminating massive diversion and overprescribing of amphetamines. Because of intense public pressure in the late 1960s and early 1970s Congress and BNDD reacted by severely restricting production and distribution of amphetamines throughout the legitimate drug industry and by requiring practitioners to write (not telephone) nonrefillable prescriptions for their patients.

The reaction to overprescribing and extensive diversion of amphetamines also manifested itself in state legislation. Thirty-eight states and three territories adopted the Uniform Controlled Substances Act within the year and a half following the Federal law's adoption. These laws, which parallel the Federal Act, are designed to form an interlocking regulatory enforcement mechanism with the Federal government by giving states comparable authority to the Federal government. Through its new, sophisticated computer operation BNDD plans to work with the states to trace distribution of amphetamines throughout the country in order to pinpoint and cut off diversion.

What does the future hold? Should these new procedures and controls prove inadequate, prescribing of amphetamines might be entirely halted except for special clinics which would administer to the needs of narcoleptics and those hyperkinetic children who are deemed to need such treatment. Already several states have either passed legislation or are considering legislation to do just this. Hopefully, such procedures will be unnecessary. Legal restrictions on medical practice may inhibit potential useful experimentation and innovation despite the exemption which formal research is usually granted.

What can be done short of these extreme measures? Medical students and physicians should become more fully informed regarding the real values and risks of the stimulants. Prescribing in quantities greater than 100 should be avoided and dosage units should contain no more than 5 milligrams of amphetamine or methamphetamine per tablet or capsule (with appropriate dosages for related amphetamine-like substances whose potency differs from amphetamine). Tablet and capsule preparations containing small quantities of phenothiazines in combination with amphetamines should be carefully studied since it appears that such combinations may not adversely affect the action of the amphetamines and may be less prone to abuse because the cumulative effect of the phenothiazine becomes relatively more prominent when large quantities of this combination are used. Such changes, if widely accepted, would reduce the likelihood of medical misuse and diversion from legitimate channels.

Amphetamines are substances with significant potential for abuse. Both voluntary action on the part of doctors and drug companies as well as restrictions on prescribing and manufacture are needed to minimize accidental dependence and cut off a major source of supply to the illicit market.

REFERENCES

Baumgartner, Kenneth, and Michael Morrell, 1972. "Pharmaceutical industry regulation by the Department of Justice," *Syracuse Law Review* 23:785-815.

Benzedrine Sulfate "Pep Pills," 1937. Editorial in *Journal of the American Medical Association.* Vol. 108, pp. 1973-74.

Bradley, C. 1937. The behavior of children receiving benzedrine. *American Journal of Psychiatry* 94:577-85.

Brill, H., and Hirose, T. 1969. The rise and fall of a methamphetamine epidemic: Japan 1945-55. *Seminars in Psychiatry* 1:179-94.

Cole, J. 1969. The amphetamines in child psychiatry: a review. *Seminars in Psychiatry* 1:174-79.

Connell, P. H. 1958. *Amphetamine psychosis.* London: Chapman and Hall, Ltd.

Durrin, K. A. 1970. Federal regulation to prevent diversion from legitimate channels. Paper read, April 8, 1970, at Southern Methodist University, Dallas, Texas.

Ellinwood, E. H. 1971. Assault and homicide associated with amphetamine
abuse. *American Journal of Psychiatry* 127:1170–1175.

Federal Register. 1971. Vol. 36, p. 9563.

———. 1972. Vol. 37, p. 3194.

———. 1973. Vol. 38.

Huff, B. B. 1970. *Physicians' desk reference to pharmaceutical specialties
and biologicals.* Oradell, N.Y.: Medical Economics, Inc.

Leake, C. 1958. *The amphetamines.* Springfield, Ill.: Charles C Thomas,
Publisher.

Penick, S. B. 1969. Amphetamines in obesity. *Seminars in Psychiatry*
1:144–62.

Peoples, S. A., and Guttman, E. 1936. Hypertension produced with benzedrine. *Lancet* 1:1107–9.

Presidential Reorganization Plan. U.S. Congress 1969 Presidential Message
to Congress.

United States Code. 1973. Title 21, sec. 801–966.

U.S. Congress. 1970. Comprehensive Drug Abuse Prevention and Control
Act of 1970. U.S. Code, Congressional and Administrative News, 91st
Cong. 2d Sess. 1970, pp. 4567–4657.

———. 1965. Drug Abuse Control Amendments to Food, Drug and Cosmetic Act. U.S. Code, Congressional and Administrative News, 89th
Cong., 1st Sess., 1965, pp. 1895–1909.

von Hoffman, N. 1970. Pep talk. *Washington Post,* July 22, 1970, sect. b,
p. 1.

Wheatley, D. 1969. Amphetamines in general practice: their use in depression and anxiety. *Seminars in Psychiatry* 1:163–73.

an analysis of amphetamine toxicity and patterns of use

J. Fred E. Shick, M.D. / David E. Smith, M.D. / Donald R. Wesson, M.D.

introduction

In the midst of the recent drug-abuse epidemic (Shick and Freedman 1973) there has been a concomitant increase in the use, misuse, and frank abuse of central nervous system stimulants such as the amphetamines, and, even more recently, cocaine has become widely available. Although in terms of adverse outcomes and extent of abuse the largest drug problem in the country is still alcoholism, amphetamine abuse represents an as yet incompletely assessed fraction of the total drug-abuse problem. Called "speed" by the younger generation, this drug has limited therapeutic use and is indicated primarily in the treatment of the rare syndromes of hyperkinesis and narcolepsy. In the late 1960s dramatic stories describing drug-using subcultures, such as the Haight-Ashbury district of San Francisco, stressed the violence associated with "speed scenes" and alerted America's dominant culture to the idea that a significant and serious new drug problem existed. The extent to which these accounts affected the magnitude of the "problem" itself is unresearched. While the media have labeled amphetamine abuse a problem of youth, it is not confined simply to illegal drug-using subcultures such as Haight-Ashbury (San Francisco), Sunset Strip (Los Angeles), Greenwich Village (New York), etc., but may be present in all levels of society to an as yet undetermined degree. Amphetamines may be obtained illegally (as for instance in "needle cultures" of our large cities), but also they may be purchased legally initially for medical purposes and then later misused for various reasons by those who find them attractive. Persons who misuse medically prescribed amphetamines are an unresearched sector of amphetamine abusers, and those who obtain amphetamines from illegal outlets are the more visible segment. Amphetamine abuse then is cross-cultural, involving both hip and straight, young and old alike.

The history of stimulant use by Western medicine begins with Sigmund Freud, who in the early 1880s, during the time of his engagement to his future wife, obtained some cocaine from Merck to study its effects. He wrote of its history and stimulant effects (Freud 1963) and even hinted that it might be used as an anesthetic in ophthalmology—an action later discovered and described by Carl Koller and Leopold Königstein, both ophthalmologists (Jones 1953). Narrowly missing fame for the discovery of its anesthetic properties, Freud became an advocate of its stimulant properties and used it himself for a few years periodically in small doses administered orally, sent some occasionally to his betrothed (though later cautioned her against becoming dependent), tried it in treating heart disease, "nervous exhaustion," and neurasthenia, and advocated its use in morphine withdrawal. He began to understand some of the adverse consequences of continued use in high doses when his friend, Dr. Fleischl, who was dependent on morphine for the pain of a neuroma, and for whom Freud prescribed cocaine to withdraw him from morphine, became "delirious" from the high (more than a gram a day) doses he used (Jones 1953). No doubt this was the first reported case of cocaine toxic psychosis.

By 1887 it was clear to Freud that those addicted to morphine could become addicted also to cocaine, and he withdrew his earlier recommendations, implicated the use of hypodermic injection (then used subcutaneously) as a causative factor in the addiction, described the toxic effects of high doses, and implied that personality factors in addicts were responsible for addiction (Freud 1963). Some physicians had accused Freud of unleashing "the third scourge of humanity" the other two being alcohol and morphine (Jones 1953). Thus began and ended Freud's advocacy of cocaine.

It was years later that a synthetic stimulant, amphetamine, became an agent of abuse, and long before the problem surfaced in this country other nations experienced epidemics of its abuse.

After World War II amphetamines were available in Japan on a nonprescription basis, and by 1954, when controls were placed on the drug, there were estimated to be more than 200,000 amphetamine addicts in Japan (Shick and Freedman 1973). Most of these individuals were abusing methamphetamine intravenously but in a low-dose maintenance pattern unlike the cyclical high-dose pattern popular nowadays among the youth. The manufacture of amphetamine tablets for use by the servicemen in World War II provided an ample supply. During World War II, the German, Japanese, and Allied forces distributed amphetamines to increase the "war effort." Bell and Trithowan (1961) note that "more than 72 million energy tablets were supplied to service personnel in Great Britain and much the same quantity to the United States Armed Forces." The British noted increasing oral amphetamine dependence after the war, and they followed Japan's lead by placing these stimulant drugs under control in 1957, and withdrawing nasal inhalers containing the drug from the market. However, amphetamines continued to be dispensed in England "lightheartedly" by physicians for "obesity, depression, tiredness, and anxiety" particularly in the 35- to 45-year-old group. By the early 1960s British teenagers had begun ingesting oral preparations for "kicks and thrills" particularly as sedative-amphetamine combinations. The Swedish, too, have experienced an epidemic of oral amphetamine dependence, primarily with the amphetamine derivative, phenmetrazine, dispensed largely for weight control (Bejerot 1968).

The history of America's concern over amphetamine abuse described in detail by Griffith and associates (1971) began with an editorial in the *Journal of the American Medical Association* in 1937, which noted a possibility of abuse by students who had learned about the drug from experiments being done with it at the University of Minnesota, and had obtained it for use as a "study aid" (Griffith, Davis, and Oates 1971). Little more was heard about amphetamine abuse here until 1966 when a report of intravenous and oral misuse was published which estimated that about 5,000 individuals in Oklahoma City obtained amphetamines illegally (Griffith 1966; Kramer, Fischman, and Littlefield 1967). The authors felt that intravenous use was generally in low doses and relatively infrequent. In San Francisco some physicians in the early 1960s had begun prescribing methamphetamine by self-injection for heroin abusers in an attempt to treat their heroin habit by substituting amphetamine (thought to be "nonaddicting"). Heroin abusers who had converted to the intravenous use of amphetamine tended to maintain rather stable methamphetamine habits, costing $20 to $30 per week, and showed little tendency to increase the dose (Kramer, Fischman, and Littlefield 1967; Shick, Smith, and Meyers 1970). Thus, the first incidence of intravenous abuse in this country could be thought of as a low-dose maintenance pattern.

Kramer and associates (1967) were the first to describe the high-dose cyclical pattern of intravenous abuse which reached epidemic proportions during the late 1960s. They reviewed the problem in California which seemed to appear first in the Haight-Ashbury during the "summer of love" in 1967 (Shick, Smith, and Meyers 1970) while in other parts of the country "pot and acid" were beginning to be experimented with (Smith 1970). Many habitual psychedelic users in San Francisco began to use amphetamine to treat the "psychedelic confusion" they experienced after continued LSD use (D. E. Smith 1969a). As the "speed scene" began to conflict with the "acid head" group (Smith 1969c), the original "hippie" scene in Haight-Ashbury began to disappear; these youths moved away from the neighborhood into communes and other enclaves. The ritual of "shooting up with speed" spread throughout the youthful drug-using subcultures springing up all over the nation. High school students began experimenting with speed both intravenously and orally, and particularly for some persons who had dropped out of high school the speed scene temporarily became a way of life.

Since that time drug centers such as the Haight-Ashbury have continued to attract youthful drug abusers, but intravenous methamphetamine abuse has for the most part given way to intravenous heroin and barbiturate abuse (Shick, Smith, and Meyers 1970; D. E. Smith 1969a and b; Smith, Wesson, and Lannon 1970). An illegal speed scene is a transient, unstable affair and appears to be a major door to the "downer scenes" of heroin and barbiturates. With the increased availability of heroin to middle-class youth, heroin itself has become a drug of choice for many. The intravenous use of amphetamine and heroin together or in combination with barbiturates is being reported by many drug abusers. It is reminiscent of the old "speed-ball" consisting of heroin and cocaine, popular in an earlier drug epidemic in America (Hughes and Jaffe 1971). Most recently there has been an increase in the availability of cocaine to white middle-class youth, and they have begun to use this stimulant by nasal inhalation and injection. Cocaine may produce all the toxic reactions of amphetamine, including the amphetamine psychosis, although the drug itself has a shorter duration of action than amphetamine and appears to act by a somewhat different biochemical mechanism.

Oral amphetamine abuse among adults is for many reasons usually disregarded, yet an unresearched number of people *depend* upon the drugs for weight control or relief from general lassitude. No one likes to recognize the problem that the medical prescription of these drugs poses. There is discussion of issues such as whether patients should be warned by their physicians that dependence may develop or that the depression which may ensue after discontinuing a round of diet pills is part of a drug-withdrawal phenomenon. Some irresponsible physicians ("pathological prescribers" or "script doctors") are known among drug users for prescribing amphetamines with little or no indication, and abusers often obtain their supplies from them for the price of an office visit. Discussion has recently begun over the use of amphetamines in the treatment of the hyperkinetic child (Eisenberg 1971 and 1972; Fish 1971; Freedman 1971; Mendelson, Johnson, and Stewart 1971; Menkes, Rowe, and Menkes 1967; Weiss et al. 1971). Furthermore, the use of amphetamines by athletes to improve their physical performance—particularly during the last two Olympic Games—has added to the amphetamine controversy. Newspaper reports have stimulated a public outcry for investigation into the indiscriminate use of these drugs without close medical supervision. At present it is impossible to determine how widespread the unsupervised use is, and final evaluation must await the results of responsible investigation.

Thus amphetamine abuse is one problem which bridges the generation gap. The recent commotion generated by the media, which alerted the public that large numbers of white middle-class youth were using heroin, overshadowed the transient concern about amphetamine. Yet the problem still lingers. The history of control of this drug in the U.S. has been reviewed by Griffith, Davis, and Oates (1971). Recently the BNDD and some states have changed their laws to place amphetamine under the controls already adopted for narcotics, and production quotas have been imposed. As a result many dependent people have found it more difficult to obtain the drug and have purchased it through illegal channels, substituted other drugs, or appeared in psychiatric clinics requesting either the drug or treatment for their dependence. The intravenous abuse of amphetamine among youth represents only the peak of a larger pyramid of amphetamine experimentation, self-treatment use, and compulsive use among adults as well as youth. Dependence upon diet pills, "awakeners," and "pep pills" by adults is just as surely abuse of the amphetamines as intravenous injection by "speed freaks," and differs only in pattern. It is these differing patterns of amphetamine abuse which we will delineate in this paper as well as discussing the possible toxic effects, both acute and chronic, attendant with these patterns.

the extent of amphetamine abuse

Alcoholism is the number one drug-abuse problem in this country: the total number of heroin, barbiturate, and amphetamine abusers does not equal even a tenth of the number of alcoholics. The publicity accorded the intravenous abuse patterns ("speed freaks") suggested that (in terms of numbers using the drugs) oral abuse was less of a problem than intravenous abuse. In terms of adverse reactions, intravenous use may be the greater problem. Oral abuse is more common than intravenous abuse, which is often preceded by extensive experimentation with the oral preparations. No studies have assessed whether the use of amphetamines obtained through legal channels is of greater magnitude than the illegal purchase of these drugs. It may be that large segments of the oral amphetamine-abuse problem are hidden in the respectable middle-class confines of the dominant culture. Our clinical impression is that the abuse of amphetamine is prevalent among adults as well as among the youth, and intravenous abuse appears less common than experimental use or habitual use of the oral preparations.

Obtaining an accurate estimate of the extent of amphetamine abuse is complicated by the wide variation in the (largely unassessed) validity and reliability of the data-gathering methodology among the various surveys, each of which draws its sample from a different population sector. Furthermore, most studies surveying amphetamine misuse have failed to distinguish between oral and intravenous routes of administration. This is a crucial variable to assess, particularly when surveying amphetamine abusers, since the different routes of administration imply differences not only in the subjective effects experienced by users but also in the patterns of use, different motivations for using, social milieus of the user, and degree of toxic effects. They may also reflect differences in degree of involvement in the drug abuse scene, and in therapeutic and prognostic implications. Other problems implicit in the epidemiological study of drug abuse—problems of perspective, focus, methodology, definition, and usefulness—have been discussed more fully elsewhere (Shick and Freedman 1973).

Comparisons between the studies are difficult. Some studies measure incidence, others prevalence, few assess duration, frequency and intensity of use (National Commission on Marijuana and Drug Abuse 1972), and furthermore the studies survey different population sectors and utilize sampling methods which often do not allow extrapolation to the universe from which the sample is drawn (Berg 1970; DeAlarcon 1972a; Robbins et al. 1968; Shick and Freedman 1973). One review (Berg 1970) of the many survey studies available indicated that the percentage of persons who have tried amphetamines at least once, intravenously or orally, varies from 27% among the students in a Northwestern medical school to 60% among the members of "hippie subcultures" in the Eastern and Western metropolitan areas. Lower figures of 11% (of undergraduate and graduate students in a Western university) and 20% (of students in a Western high school district) were also described in this study. The percentage of high school students who have tried amphetamines generally increases with age—the greatest numbers being among the senior students—and tends to vary with the type of community from which the school draws its students (Berg 1970). Illicit use by students is most prevalent in urban high schools, less prevalent in schools in smaller cities, and lowest in schools in rural areas (Berg 1970). One early study (Shick, Smith, and Meyers 1970) sampling the Haight-Ashbury in 1967 indicated that experience with oral preparations is commoner than experience with intravenous preparations, and that most of the intravenous users had had previous experience with oral amphetamines. From 1967 through 1968 about 7–12% of the population of the Haight-Ashbury were habitually using amphetamines—almost exclusively intravenously. Since that time the amount of intravenous experimentation has increased, yet chronic patterns of intravenous abuse now tend to be with heroin and barbiturates (Smith, Wesson, and Lannon 1970).

The national survey conducted for the National Commission on Marijuana and Drug Abuse (NCMDA 1972) reported that 6% of American youth (ages 12 through 17) and 13% of adults had some experience with stimulants, and 4% of youth and 5% of adults had used stimulant drugs obtained by prescription at least once for non-medical reasons. By contrast, 24% of youth and 53% of adults presently use alcohol. Stimulants were used regularly by 2% of adults, generally in the 18- to 34-year-old-range. Cocaine had been tried by 3% of adults and 1.5% of the youth. Stimulant use was greater among better educated adults who resided in metropolitan areas and lived in the West. The same 1972 survey sampled American students and found that 9% of junior high school students, 19% of senior high school students, and 24% of college students had taken stimulants at least once. Trend data indicated that student stimulant use had increased 41% between 1970 and 1972, indicating a rise in consumption among college students followed in about one year by a rise in use among secondary students. Fourteen percent of secondary school students and 11% of college students used stimulants once a week or more, often concurrently with other drugs. On the other hand, the data suggested that "student drug use although now beginning earlier than in the past, ordinarily remains a short-lived phenomena regardless of the age or time of onset, and most students terminate or significantly reduce the frequency and intensity of their drug use, except for alcohol and marijuana when they reach college."

A survey (Zaks et al. 1969) of the Yippies in Lincoln Park during the Chicago Democratic Convention in 1968 revealed that both oral and intravenous amphetamine use was common among the sample, though the use of these drugs was "not characteristic of the majority of the subjects." Twenty-eight percent of the sample claimed regular weekly use of Dexedrine (probably orally) and 14% claimed regular weekly use of methamphetamine (presumably intravenously). Women tended to use both drugs more frequently than men in this study, and experience with amphetamines was particularly characteristic of the younger (13- to 16-year-old) subjects. The increased tendency to use the drug that is sold in the street as "mescaline" and which often is STP, a psychotomimetic amphetamine derivative (Shick and Smith 1973), was also noted by this study.

Some misuse of amphetamine occurs in patients who obtain the drug from medical practitioners, primarily to treat their obesity or states of ill-feelings such as depression. Recent studies (Mellinger, Balter, and Manheimer 1971; Gottschalk et al. 1971; Parry et al. 1973) have focused the use of psychoactive drugs. Mellinger remarks on the tendency, particularly among youth, to circumvent medical agencies to obtain—either through illicit channels or through the use of over-the-counter preparations—various psychoactive drugs for self-medication, and to increasingly disregard advice from medical agencies about toxic effects and long-term consequences of such misuse. The use of stimulants ranked first in prevalence among adult men and women in this San Francisco adult population.

Hawks et al. (1969) discusses the extent of amphetamine abuse in Great Britain. From a selected sample of methamphetamine abusers, he describes their demographic data, personal history, drug history, the origins of their supply, the progression to other drugs and patterns of use, and some of the toxic effects experienced by this sample.

There have been no studies which have assessed the natural history of the disorder in terms of morbidity and mortality, and generalizations about the trends of amphetamine use are made up largely of speculation and a few anecdotal accounts.

patterns of use

Drugs may be used in various *patterns* determined by a number of factors—political, legal, cultural, and economic influences, small and large group phenomena, personal goals, psychic structure and dynamics, family and interpersonal peer group dynamics, reinforcement effects of the drug, ritual and social setting, as well as by drug factors such as abuse potential, tolerance, withdrawal effects, and adverse reactions (Shick and Freedman 1973). All of these factors interact to determine when a person begins to use a drug, which drug he uses, and when he terminates his drug use or progresses to a different pattern. It is important to try to distinguish use from abuse, to discuss use in terms of relative risks, and among various patterns of use. In any individual these distinctions may be blurred at times.

Drug use begins as an elective experimental trial which terminates with the user either rejecting continued use of the drug or adopting another pattern of use. He may continue to use the drug either for recreational and social purposes; task-specific, self-limited circumstantial-situational use; attempts at self-medication; or high frequency, high intensity compulsive use (Shick and Freedman 1973; Meyers, Jawetz, and Goldfien 1968; NCMDA 1972). Amphetamine is sometimes used either orally or intravenously to counteract the effects of other drugs, and often—once a pattern of continued use is established—to ameliorate the effects of amphetamine abstinence. It may be used electively in low doses orally administered to enhance physical or emotional performance, or it may be used in high doses, either orally or intravenously, to produce euphoria. Many people adopt the habit of occasional amphetamine use in low doses orally —for instance, to study for an exam or for "treatment" of their obesity. This may be considered recreational or circumstantial-situational use as long as it does not progress to intensified use and episodic abuse with adverse consequences. Experimental intravenous use exists primarily within the youthful sectors of the population, is most common among those who have dropped out of school, and tends to be a sign of extensive involvement in the drug-using subculture.

The use of the term *abuse* has generally superseded the use of the term *addiction* in an effort to remove drug use from the moralistic arena, yet the term abuse has gradually come to imply societal disapproval (NCMDA 1972). One person's definition of abuse may not be another's—the term has very personal meanings for both the investigator and his subjects. The decision that a person is "abusing" a drug often depends upon the weight an investigator gives to the consequences and outcome of a subject's use; the frequency, duration, intensity and amount of use, and the political and social orientation of the investigator or his subject (Shick and Freedman 1973). The terms addiction, abuse, and dependence do not communicate the same meaning to everyone. The precise distinction is not necessarily explicit—nor always conscious to the investigator— and terms may "bear the burden of cultural attitude and overtones which are never quite explicit" (Shick and Freedman 1973). One definition for drug abuse, that is, use of a drug to the point where it interferes with one's health, social, personal, or economic functioning, has been discussed elsewhere (Meyers, Jawetz, and Goldfien 1968; Shick, Smith, and Meyers 1970) and rests upon decisions regarding the frequency and intensity of the use relative to anticipated consequences and outcomes of such use (Shick and Freedman 1973). This definition has certain weaknesses, however, since such relationships vary from individual to individual, and a person may experience a lasting consequence from even a single episode of drug experimentation; thus the experience of an adverse effect implies nothing about a person's "dependency" on a particular drug. The pattern of use of one drug does not necessarily imply that other drugs are used in the same pattern, although they may be. If two drugs are used compulsively, either concurrently or at different times, we term this *multiple drug abuse* (NCMDA 1972; Shick, Smith, and Meyers 1970; Shick and Freedman 1973), which is characteristic of many drug users. Some studies have attempted to distinguish use from abuse on the basis of whether drugs are used under "medical supervision." The use of amphetamines under medical auspices, however, cannot be perfectly supervised, and some doctors' patients may actually abuse the drug, particularly "diet pills." Although most personal use of ethical or proprietary drugs is time-limited and conservative (Parry, et al. 1973), some practitioners prescribe amphetamine equivalents (e.g., Tenwate or Preludin) indiscriminately for weight reduction, cajoled by pharmaceutical advertisements which claim they are innocuous "appetite depressants" without the side effects of amphetamines. In fact, they are central nervous system stimulants with approximately the same effect and complications as the amphetamines in equivalent dosage. If taken according to the way they are prescribed, the risk of dependence and side effects is quite low. But "medically supervised" amphetamine use can be for some susceptible individuals as dangerous as illicit use and can often be the beginning of a long history of drug dependence by those prone to it.

Various authors have attempted to define who is at risk to abuse drugs by studying demographic and personal variables, constructing "willingness" scales, assessing motivations for use, and investigating precipitants and environmental stress surrounding the onset of use or abuse (Shick and Freedman 1973). Bell (1972) has recently described the precipitants (defined as a new circumstance associated in time with the onset of amphetamine addiction which has some deeper psychological significance to the patient) surrounding a person's progression to the abuse of amphetamine. He discovered precipitants in 34 of 40 cases of amphetamine abuse closely linked in time to the onset of addiction and which, in 12 cases, resulted in a "change in the patient's environment, allowing ready access to amphetamine for the first time." He found the precipitants to be commonplace, yet stressful life events of two main types: rejection or separation from a loved or admired object, and the transition to a more demanding adult role (e.g., marriage, promotion). Both seem to resonate with important factors in the patient's psychological genetics and dynamics.

Within the compulsive pattern of amphetamine use lie two distinct subpatterns: a high-dose cyclical pattern and a low-dose maintenance pattern. At the present time the former is almost exclusively intravenous and the latter primarily oral. The cyclical nature of the high-dose pattern of use appears to stem from the high doses used and the user's experience of exhaustion and adverse effects (such as amphetamine psychosis), which force him to discontinue amphetamine use for a short while (D. E. Smith 1969a and b; Smith and Fischer 1969 and 1970). This same cyclical pattern is seen in experimental animals when they are allowed to inject the drug intravenously *ad lib*, and the metabolic and biochemical determinants are as yet undefined.

oral amphetamine abuse (low-dose maintenance pattern)

Oral amphetamines were often indiscriminately prescribed for depression and weight control before physicians became aware of their abuse potential. Although tried as a treatment for depression, amphetamines were soon abandoned by physicians as the MAO (monoamine oxidase) inhibitors and the tricyclic antidepressants proved to have less abuse potential and a greater effectiveness with fewer hazards over the long term. Amphetamine use in the treatment of certain hyperkinetic children is still advocated although such use is controversial (Eisenberg 1971; Fish 1971; Freedman 1971; Kornetsky 1970). Among these children it seems to have a "paradoxical" effect of calming the hyperkinetic syndrome, rather than inducing hyperactivity as it does in "normal" subjects, and yet the bio-behavioral reasons behind this seemingly paradoxical effect remain largely unknown. At the present time the largest quantities of oral amphetamines are prescribed for weight reduction—although many clinicians feel that the side effects, adverse reactions, and abuse potential of the drug or its relatives far outweigh its advantages, and that strict dietary control without drugs or the short-term use of amphetamines for weight control are the recommended approaches.

Users experience subjective effects after oral use which differ from those experienced after intravenous amphetamine injection. Central nervous system stimulation is delayed due to gastric absorption for 30 to 40 minutes after swallowing the drug. Thus there is no "rush" or "flash" as with intravenous use; instead, euphoria and stimulation increase gradually as more drug enters the bloodstream. Small amounts of the drug do increase the performance of certain motor tasks such as swimming, and it is sometimes speculated that intellectual function is similarly enhanced with low doses, although this has never been proven (Kosman and Unna 1968). Different degrees of peripheral autonomic stimulation, such as sweating, dry mouth, and dilated pupils, seem to appear with different frequencies depending upon the type of amphetamine or amphetamine derivative used, although there have been negative findings in this regard (Martin et al. 1971). For example, Ritalin (methylphenidate), which is a synthetic stimulant, is thought to produce very few peripheral side effects, whereas Biphetamine (d,1-amphetamine), is thought to produce many side effects even at low doses. The occurrence of such side effects is also a dose-related phenomenon. Euphoria and feelings of well-being are increased as the dosage increases, and side effects of tremulousness, wakefulness, and appetite suppression also increase with dose. Thus the usual picture of the central low-dose effects of oral amphetamine use includes a gradual elevation in mood and decreased fatigue, accompanied by side effects depending upon both the dose and probably the type of preparation used (Kosman and Unna 1968). Furthermore the way a user manages or interprets the experience and its consequences and outcome depends on things besides drug effects (e.g., social and group phenomena, reinforcement effects of the drug and the setting, and intrapsychic determinants).

Although a pattern of oral abuse can occasionally be traced to a physician's initial prescription for weight reduction—particularly among young women—a study by Hawks et al. (1969) shows that even among individuals using the drug in a low-dose maintenance pattern, friends or siblings were most often the first people to introduce the user to the drug. Hawks found that among these users an average of seven and a half weeks elapsed from their first introduction to the drug to its daily use.

Compulsive oral amphetamine use is often considered a problem of the middle-aged, particularly housewives, executives who work long hours, and those who travel extensively by air and use drugs to readjust their sleep-wake cycle. Such individuals tend to maintain a rather stable daily intake of amphetamines over long periods of time, which characterizes this low-dose maintenance pattern. The Rolling Stones have immortalized housewives with monotonous daily lives who use the drug as "Mother's Little Helper." There are individuals such as executives, politicians during a campaign, or rock musicians who use the drug daily, yet maintain their functioning for a while in competitive, "stressful" jobs.

Chronic amphetamine users report feeling stronger, calmer, more confident and decisive. Patients say, "I felt I could do anything I cared to," or, "You feel as though you can master anything; that nothing is impossible to attain" (Fischmann 1968). All too often the user finds the pills are a necessity to maintain normal daily function. Commonly a pattern emerges of taking an "upper" in the morning and a "downer" such as alcohol or a sleeping pill in the evening to get to sleep. Often sedatives and amphetamines are taken together, since the sedative tends to counteract the tremulousness and nervousness. This is the rationale for marketing amphetamine-sedative combinations such as Dexamyl (d-amphetamine and amobarbital). The mixture of alcohol and barbiturates can be lethal, and may be the agents in conscious or unconscious suicide attempts.

Use for self-medication to treat various states of ill-feeling is common. Some unhappy people will continue to maintain their excessive weight primarily in order to obtain from their doctor the "diet pill" which relieves their generalized dysphoria more than it controls their weight. Amphetamines may be used to ameliorate primary depression, or the depression which results from discontinuing use (discussed under abstinence syndrome) may provoke continued use. Some schizophrenics will take the drug in a low-dose maintenance pattern to relieve their sense of isolation; yet in others it may exacerbate psychotic thinking. Oral amphetamine abuse exists also among youth, who take somewhat larger doses for elation or euphoria, in episodic abuse patterns over the weekend or at night. Such users generally extend their drug use to include other drugs and often become "multiple drug abusers." It is becoming apparent, particularly in high-density drug-use areas, that oral *and* intravenous amphetamines are being used purely for recreational purposes, and often such users do not experience the adverse effects which would bring them to medical or psychiatric facilities. It may be that among these users adverse effects are being managed by their friends or the drug-using community in which they live.

intravenous amphetamine abuse (high-dose cyclical patterns)

The compulsive pattern of intravenous amphetamine abuse differs significantly from the compulsive oral pattern of low-dose maintenance previously described. Furthermore, that oral preparations such as Desoxyn may be used for intravenous injection often goes unrecognized. Particularly where crystalline methamphetamine is less available, "pill soaking" of amphetamine tablets occurs. Dextroamphetamine is less soluble than methamphetamine, but sufficient amounts dissolve to permit intravenous injection.

Within this pattern, after an initial experimental phase, the user injects an amphetamine preparation many times a day in progressively higher doses. Intravenous injection immediately produces a "flash" or "rush" which is sometimes characterized as a "total body orgasm" and includes tingling in the head and extremities, tachycardia, and the feeling that it "takes my breath away" (R. C. Smith 1969b). Hawks et al. (1969) has described the intramuscular injection he found among some of his users—an occurrence seldom seen in this country. The mythology within the "needle culture" implies that different subjective "rushes" depend upon *contaminants* in the illegally manufactured "crystal" (methamphetamine) (R. C. Smith 1969a and b), for instance, the aldehydes or esters which may be present in the crudely manufactured drugs, or in the substance with which the drug is cut. After the first few minutes, the rush decreases and blends imperceptibly into a level of central stimulation indistinguishable from that produced by the oral administration of amphetamines. This lasts for several hours, depending on the duration of the effect of the drug and on the dose used. The "comedown," referred to as "crashing," when the effects wear off, is universally described as unpleasant by users. They may try to counteract the effect by injecting more stimulants or to soften the "crash" with heroin or barbiturates. This pattern of injecting the drug every two to six hours is repeated time and again until the user discontinues the drug for one of several reasons. He often becomes simply exhausted, he may be arrested, his supply of the drug may run out, or an amphetamine psychosis or other adverse effects may develop which force him to terminate his drug use for a while.

When and for what reasons this pattern of high-dose cyclical use stops is unresolved. Long-term studies of the natural history of intravenous amphetamine abuse and its consequences and outcomes in terms of morbidity and mortality are needed. Clinical impressions indicate that mortality within a two-year period after the assumption of a high-dose cyclical pattern of intravenous amphetamine use is rather high, although the cause of death is often not directly from the drug, but rather from a resultant of amphetamine abuse: violence, hepatitis, malnutrition, or a heroin or barbiturate overdose when these drugs are used in a later phase. A small percentage of users get some sort of rehabilitation, either in a hospital setting or in outpatient clinics, and usually a user must separate from his environment of drug-using friends in order to maintain abstinence. The user often goes on to try other drugs intravenously (e.g., concentrating exclusively on heroin or barbiturates), or he may begin an oral maintenance pattern of psychedelic abuse, which is discussed elsewhere (Shick and Smith 1973).

acute and chronic toxicity of intravenous and oral amphetamine use

Oral and intravenous use may result in the same chronic toxic effects. Although some, like serum hepatitis, occur as a consequence only of intravenous use, certainly many more toxic reactions are seen with intravenous use because of the extremely large doses used. Treatment is discussed where relevant.

acute amphetamine toxicity

Goodman and Gilman (1970) list the acute toxic effects as restlessness, tremor, talkativeness, irritability, insomnia, euphoria, anorexia, assaultiveness, anxiety, delirium, hallucination, panic states, paranoid ideation, palpitation, cardiac arrhythmias, hypertension or hypotension, circulatory collapse, dry mouth, nausea, vomiting, labile affect, abdominal cramps, convulsions, and coma. The toxic dose varies widely and may occur as an idiosyncratic reaction after as little as 2 mg. but more usually in excess of 30 to 60 mg. (Goodman and Gilman 1970). Some individuals may experience an acute "paradoxical" effect of increased depression, instead of the more usual euphoria and elation.

overdose and acute anxiety reaction

Some of the more important acute toxic effects occur after overdosing ("overamping") which often occurs with intravenous administration. This syndrome, which is described in detail by Kramer, Fischman, and Littlefield (1967), may result in chest pain, immobilization, and even brief comatose states, and may lead the user to inject another drug to try to counteract the amphetamine effect. Individual "shootouts" between users are described by R. C. Smith (1969b).

Accidental overdoses in children have been described by Espelin and Done (1969), and death in these cases resulted from high fever, convulsions, coma, and circulatory collapse (Zalis, Lundburg, and Knutson 1967). Yet among deliberate users death from an overdose of amphetamine alone is seldom seen (Cravey and Baselt 1968; Weiss, Raskino, and Morganstern 1970), and thus the phrase, "speed kills," is often misunderstood. Chronic toxicity of amphetamine rather than acute overdose accounts for much of the mortality among abusers. The use of other drugs may also play a role.

Acute overdoses are best treated with chlorpromazine (although drugs such as diazepam or thiothixene [Weissman 1968] may be used), and even mild doses (50 to 100 mg. I.M.) may sedate the individual enough so that the acute effect of the overdose can be allowed to run its course. Where hyperpyrexia is a problem, hypothermia may be instituted (Espelin and Done 1969). When amphetamine-barbiturate combinations have been taken, barbiturate intoxication or overdose may supervene after the amphetamine effect has worn off. Adrenergic blocking agents may be used in conjunction with a phenothiazine in cases where there is severe hypertension, although the hypotensive effects of chlorpromazine should be taken into account (Espelin and Done 1969).

Smith and Fischer (1969) and Kramer, Fischman, and Littlefield (1967) discuss the acute anxiety reaction which may accompany large doses of intravenous amphetamine, particularly in inexperienced users. The user may become acutely anxious and focus his attention on the physical symptomatology of the sympathomimetic effect, such as the profuse sweating, photophobia, or tachycardia, which accompanies high doses. The anxiety may be quite severe, and often brings the user to medical attention particularly where a "speed culture" has not yet evolved who would "talk down" their own members. Fear of loss of control is one important dynamic generally involved. Psychiatric symptomatology is often exaggerated under the effects of the drug, and the effects of the social setting in which the drug is taken and the influence of the user's associates play an important role in the production, interpretation and outcome of the acute anxiety reaction.

chronic amphetamine toxicity

With sustained use, any of the acute toxic effects listed above may occur; but some of the more important chronic effects are discussed below.

tolerance

Tolerance to a wide variety of central nervous system (CNS) effects is evident in high-dose users (Kramer, Fischman, and Littlefield 1967; D. E. Smith 1969a and b; R. C. Smith 1969b). Abusers become tolerant to the awakening effect of the drug and report injecting increasing amounts up to hundreds of times the clinical dose in order to remain awake.

Monkeys gradually made tolerant to increasing amounts of intravenously administered methamphetamine on a chronic schedule every 3 hours become tolerant to all the effects except the stereotypic behavior (Fischmann and Schuster 1973). Stereotypic behavior in humans is visible in jaw grinding and formications ("crank bugs") which produce continued scratching of the body.

Tolerance has been shown to exist for weeks in animals after withdrawal (Kosman and Unna 1968). Although in animals there is evidence that the stimulating effect of d,1-amphetamine did not decrease with repeated administration, the chronic administration of methamphetamine in animals leads to a depression of activity (Kosman and Unna 1968). Similarly in human subjects repeated administration of dextroamphetamine (and STP, a psychedelic related to the amphetamines) leads to a reduction in activity, apathy, and withdrawal (Griffith et al. 1972; Shick and Smith 1973). The exact biochemical mechanisms involved in the development of tolerance to amphetamine are, for the most part, unknown.

abstinence syndrome

Abstinence phenomena were not seen after abrupt discontinuation of chronically administered amphetamine in monkeys (Fischmann and Schuster 1973), and the precise description of such a state in humans and the factors involved awaits further research. For many years, the consensus of medical opinion was that amphetamines were not addicting because of the absence of a withdrawal syndrome. Part of the problem lay in the semantics of "addiction," but a greater part was the difficulty in recognizing the withdrawal syndrome because of its qualitative difference from the opiate or general depressant withdrawal syndromes. The amphetamine withdrawal syndrome is characterized by apathy or a generalized dysphoric mood state ("amphetamine blues"), psychomotor retardation, and sleep disturbances which may last for weeks to months. This symptomatology is different from that which occurs with barbiturate or heroin withdrawal. Although there are few objective signs, subjective symptoms such as depression or dysphoric moods may be severe. This can occur after either oral or intravenous use and generally goes untreated. It is this depression which users feel is the stimulus for resuming a new round of amphetamine use, in an effort to counteract the dysphoria. The amphetamine user continues to shoot up for fear of the "crash" much as the heroin user continues to increase his habit in part to avoid the withdrawal. Since these symptoms may also be present in depression from other causes, careful clinical evaluation of the preamphetamine psychopathology is important. Furthermore, the fact that suicides have occurred during amphetamine withdrawal is part of the rationale for slow withdrawal in a controlled environment.

Sedative overdose is occasionally seen among abusers when they try to treat the acute amphetamine withdrawal, and it may occur when practitioners treat the acute amphetamine intoxication with large doses of sedatives. So much barbiturate is required to counteract the effects of the amphetamine intoxication, particularly after an extended "run," that when the abrupt disappearance of the amphetamine effect occurs, the patient who is treated heavily with barbiturates often shows a profound sedative overdose. Thus, moderate use of chlorpromazine or its equivalent is recommended to treat the hyperstimulation associated with amphetamine use.

organic brain syndrome

Many users insist that chronic brain damage results from the continued use of amphetamine in high-dose cyclical patterns, but such changes have not been conclusively demonstrated in humans (Freedman 1970; Utena 1966), and chronic high dose administration to monkeys showed no indication of brain tissue damage at autopsy (Fischmann and Schuster 1973). "Measures of organicity among drug users which attempt to relate findings to a particular drug are complicated by the fact that many drugs are used, of unknown purity and composition, by various routes of administration, and generally pre-drug measures are not available. The prevalence of central nervous system pathology and objective findings among chronic amphetamine users is unassessed, and the question of how long these changes persist, whether or not they are reversible, and the extent to which they manifest themselves in behavior and thinking is unexplored" (Shick and Freedman 1973).

Freedman (1970) has critically reviewed the available reports of organicity in amphetamine users prior to 1970, explaining some of the difficulties involved in such studies and concluding, "In the light of present evidence on parahydroxylated metabolites that leave the brain slowly, it is quite possible that a reversible biochemical effect is responsible for a change in behavior of this duration. . . . Drug behavior interactions—learning under the drug state— also quite possibly are involved" (Freedman 1970).

Although Rumbaugh, Bergerson, Scanlon, et al. (1971) gave pulverized amphetamine tablets in the dose range comparable to that administered by some abusers to seven monkeys intravenously and found generalized arterial spasm in two, and focal areas of ischemia and infarction and generalized edema and ischemic nerve cell changes in the brains of the remaining five at autopsy, the findings were not confirmed when the study was replicated by other investigators (Fischmann and Schuster 1973). Similar brain changes in humans (Rumbaugh, Bergerson, Fang, et al. 1971) were inferred on the basis of abnormal cerebral arteriograms on 19 chronic users, although since other drugs had been used by these multiple drug-using subjects, the findings cannot be attributed conclusively to amphetamine. A report (Citron et al. 1970) of "necrotizing angiitis" found among abusers continues to lend suspicion that some type of tissue damage may occur, not necessarily limited to the CNS, in multiple drug abusers. The appearance of persistent central nervous system signs in drug users either on EEG, or on brain scan or neurologic exam suggests cardiovascular or infectious disease processes in the brain as a result of the intravenous abuse (Louria, Hensle, and Rose 1967).

The primary symptoms which abusers report after withdrawal are difficulty with memory and sometimes with fine motor coordination. Neurological examinations of abusers who have been withdrawn have not been reported, yet observations at Mendocino State Hospital, where amphetamine abusers were treated, indicate that all *neurological* manifestations of amphetamine toxicity including objective memory loss seem to disappear after nine months to one year of abstinence. Behavioral and personality changes, which users regard as good, often persist (Kramer, Fischman, and Littlefield 1967).

physical toxicity

Physical toxicity such as hepatitis, abscesses and secondary illnesses are common complaints for which amphetamine abusers seek medical aid, and thus, facilities which deal only in psychiatric problems may miss a fair portion of the amphetamine abusers in the community. One study at the Haight-Ashbury Free Medical Clinic (Smith and Fischer 1969 and 1970) during the height of the speed epidemic in 1967 reported that the primary physical complaint of amphetamine patients was that of general debility with malnutrition. The next most common physical difficulty was that of hepatitis, which may reach epidemic proportions within a speed scene. It is difficult to understand why abusers would share needles when the problem of hepatitis is so well known, but needle sharing is common in the speed scene; one user's comment about sharing needles and the problem of hepatitis was, "Oh, we just put the yellow guy last." Although the hepatitis contracted is often the typical serum hepatitis seen within any needle culture, the incidence of hepatitis among amphetamine abusers may be higher than that among heroin addicts. This may be a result of greater needle sharing, or of a direct toxic effect to the liver—from the methamphetamine itself, from contaminants in the illegally distributed methamphetamine—or as a result of other unknown factors.

Needle sharing is a phenomenon endemic to needle-using subcultures, and is particularly prevalent among the users of the intravenous amphetamines. One study by Howard and Borges (1971) indicated that the sharing of needles among users is a social phenomenon dictated by the pressures of group participation and the availability of needles. Most inexperienced users are given their first "hit" by friends, and females, who are particularly prone to let others "shoot them up," often voice their dislike for injecting themselves. This study suggests that "many girls are marginal to the subculture, participating somewhat reluctantly because of their ties to their boyfriends." The authors inferred that "even if fits and points were legally available, sharing the needles would continue." This phenomenon seems to be an integral part of the drug subculture for reasons that go beyond pragmatic considerations (e.g., the risk of hepatitis, or the availability of needles).

Serious involvement with intravenous amphetamine exposes the user not only to direct amphetamine toxicity, but to a wide variety of other medical hazards (Louria, Hensle, and Rose 1967), relatively independent of the drug injected, such as:

1. Serum hepatitis
2. Injection of live fungus or bacteria resulting in:
   a) Septic pulmonary emboli (infected blood clots which lodge in the lungs and which may originate from infected heart valves), or septic thrombophlebitis (an infection of the veins at an infected injection site)
   b) Endocarditis (an infection of heart valves which may be produced by either a bacteria or fungus)
   c) Peripheral obstruction of arteries in cases of intra-arterial injection and due either to injection of particulate material, or to embolization; usually associated with infection
   d) Tetanus
   e) Syphilis
   f) Malaria

Because illegally manufactured drugs are never sterile and because there is much pill-soaking to obtain amphetamine, a great deal of infection results in either cellulitis or abscesses around injection sites. There are also a great number of "sterile abscesses" which occur as a result of barbiturate injection along or in combination with amphetamine when the user misses a vein and injects the substance into the tissue. The extremely alkaline nature of the barbiturate is quite irritating to the tissue and results in a "sterile" abscess with little infection and pus.

A variety of gastrointestinal symptoms other than those of hepatitis are seen in patients with chronic amphetamine abuse. These include nausea, vomiting, and abdominal cramps, the latter occasionally being so severe that a diagnosis of appendicitis is initially entertained. Necrotizing angiitis reported in some intravenous abusers may be one cause of abdominal complaints (Citron et al. 1970). Amphetamine induced cardiorespiratory symptoms are often quite distressing to the patient. Drug-induced tachycardia is often interpreted by the user as a heart attack, and the respiratory distress after "shooting-up" interpreted as a life-threatening choking sensation. Allergic reactions to contaminants in the drug may produce asthmalike attacks. The high incidence of "crank bugs" or formications (like the "coke bugs" seen with cocaine users) contribute to a high incidence of dermatologic problems.

amphetamine psychosis

Psychosis associated with drug use can occur with many drugs both during the intoxication and occasionally for varying periods of time after the acute drug effects have disappeared. "When such [psychotic] behavior occurs with a low dose, is not associated with delirium, and extends beyond the known period of [drug] action, one suspects the presence of other factors which have predisposed the individual to such a response. Such factors may include a broad range of conscious and unconscious situational or maturational stresses—psychosocial stresses which might threaten the coping capacities of the individual . . . [and] may have been involved in the original motivation to use the drug in question" (Bowers and Freedman 1973). An extended psychotic state after an intoxication is generally thought to occur in "prepsychotic," "psychosis-prone," or "vulnerable" individuals. "Neither the nature of such vulnerability nor the role of drug effects interacting with such factors has been defined.

This judgment [that a person was prepsychotic] is always made retrospectively and involves some assumptions about schizophrenia which are unproven, including the idea that pre-schizophrenic states can be characterized and recognized. The implication in these instances that drugs play a relatively unimportant role in the psychotic symptoms may be unwarranted" (Bowers and Freedman 1973). The literature on the effects of amphetamine on schizophrenic patients has been reviewed by Bowers and Freedman (1973). The prevalence and precise description of such prolonged psychoses and their outcome among users of amphetamines awaits further research.

A toxic psychosis resembling a paranoid state has long been recognized to occur as a result of chronic amphetamine administration (Angrist and Gershon 1970; Bell 1965; Bell and Trethowan 1961; Connell 1958; Ellinwood 1967 and 1968; Jonsson and Gunne 1970; Snyder 1972). Many authors compared it to paranoid schizophrenia, and some sought symptoms by which the two could be distinguished (Bell 1965; Snyder 1972). Many investigators consider this high-dose amphetamine reaction "the closest analogue of the naturally occurring psychoses," which is supported by evidence of the specificity and clinical effectiveness of the antipsychotic compounds (e.g., chlorpromazine) to antagonize the effects of amphetamines (Bowers and Freedman 1973). Griffith and associates (1972) produced a paranoid state in all volunteer subjects by administering increasing doses of dextroamphetamine orally in a period of one to six days and found large individual differences in the dose needed to produce the psychosis. All subjects had previous diagnoses of moderate personality disorder, and all were previous amphetamine users. Whether large doses of the drug will produce a psychosis in *all* individuals is probable but still speculative, since psychosocial factors which cause some persons to choose amphetamines have not been ruled out as a contributing factor in Griffith's study. There is a close correlation of the hallucinatory experience and paranoid thinking with the blood levels of amphetamine, and the disappearance of these phenomena and amphetamine excretion levels in the urine (Angrist et al. 1969; Angrist and Gershon 1970 and 1971).

Recently Snyder (1972) has discussed the amphetamine psychosis in detail and has examined its similarities and differences to paranoid schizophrenia, cocaine psychosis, alcoholic hallucinosis, psychedelic drug states, and psychoses attributed to levodopa, MAO inhibitors and tricyclic antidepressants. He has discussed a model of the neurochemical mechanisms which may be involved in producing the amphetamine-induced paranoid state in terms of the dopamine and norepinepherine neuronal interactions (Snyder 1972; Snyder et al. 1970).

At times it is difficult to distinguish between amphetamine psychosis and paranoid schizophrenia, since both may occur with clear consciousness and intact orientation. Rockwell and Ostwalt (1968) determined amphetamine in the urine by chromatography of random psychiatric hospital admissions, and found amphetamine use in 15% of these admissions. Usually such persons were diagnosed as schizophrenic. Since only half of these patients had admitted to amphetamine use, drug use was at times overlooked. The differential diagnosis of paranoid schizophrenia from amphetamine psychosis rests on observance over time or determination of amphetamine in the urine. The true amphetamine psychosis is a transient affair, disappearing upon abstinence. The occurrence of stereotyped behavior (Randrup and Munkvad 1970) and the report of increased sexual activity is suggestive of amphetamine psychosis (Snyder 1972). The appearance of a paranoid schizophreniform state which clears shortly after admission to a hospital should suggest an amphetamine psychosis, particularly if associated with hypertension, hypersexuality, or stereotyped behavior and if found in people who have a history of the use of diet pills or multiple drug abuse. Although patients with amphetamine psychosis often present with visual hallucinations which are not typical for paranoid schizophrenia, visual hallucinations are not universally found (Griffith et al. 1972) and tend to occur more often than previously thought in schizophrenia (Goodwin, Alderson, and Rosenthal 1971). Furthermore a differential resting upon the presence or absence of a thought disorder is not diagnostic either (Griffith et al. 1972).

Abusers remain continually awake for days at a time and—although a lack of REM sleep was proposed to account for the etiology of the psychosis—the study of Griffith et al. (1972) indicates that sleep deprivation alone does not account for the phenomenon. The psychosis does not appear to be a withdrawal phenomenon like the delirium of sedative withdrawal (e.g., alcoholic D.T.'s), though transient delirium may be seen rarely with extreme doses (Angrist and Gershon 1971 and 1970). More often a delirium picture is the result of other drugs such as barbiturates which are taken in conjunction with the amphetamine.

The treatment of the psychosis is abstinence, and phenothiazine tranquilizers are clinically effective and help control agitation. The stereotyped behavior in amphetamine psychosis such as compulsive jaw grinding or repetitive thoughts or acts seems to be mediated by a different brain mechanism (dopamine fibers) from that responsible for the acute intoxication (norepinepherine fibers), and haldoperidol has been said to be particularly useful in controlling stereotyped behavior, though it has not been tried in amphetamine psychosis (Snyder 1972; Snyder et al. 1970).

sex and violence

The occurrence of violence within the speed scene is well documented (Carey and Mandel 1968; Scott and Buckell 1971; R. C. Smith 1969a and b). Bach-y-rita and associates (1971) studied 130 violent patients manifesting episodic dyscontrol and noted that chronic amphetamine use played a role in 12 of them. Ellinwood (1971) studied 13 persons who committed homicide while intoxicated with amphetamine, and found that the paranoid thinking, panic, emotional lability, and lowered impulse control associated with amphetamine abuse contributed to the events leading to the homicidal act. Certainly many factors are involved including the pervasive paranoia in abusers due both to amphetamine psychosis and the illegal acts surrounding much of their lives. An additional factor may be a human analogy to "aggregate toxicity" observed in rats when, as they are given increasing doses of amphetamine, some are caged together and others caged alone (Fischer et al. 1969). Many more rats die with sublethal doses when they are caged together, and the increased mortality is due to the aggressiveness generated by the amphetamine and expressed as the rats attack and kill each other. When caged alone higher doses may be given without being lethal. We may be seeing a repeat of aggregate toxicity of amphetamine on a human scale particularly where abusers live together or in close proximity as at the Haight Street Hotel, another "flash house" (Carey and Mandel 1968; R. C. Smith 1969a and b), termed the "Crystal Palace" by speed freaks.

Tinklenberg (1972 and 1973) has recently studied the available literature on drugs and crime. "A large number of studies indicate that alcohol, the most widely used drug in the world, is clearly linked with violent crime. . . . An increasing amount of data links barbiturate users with criminal activity, especially assaultive crimes. In a recent large-scale study, the users of either amphetamines or barbiturates were more likely to be arrested for criminal homicide, forcible rape, or aggravated assault than were the users of heroin, cocaine, marijuana, hashish, tranquilizers, psychedelics, methadone, and special substances. However, amphetamine and barbiturate users were no more likely to be charged with violent crimes than were individuals who were identified as non-drug users, a category that probably included alcohol users." He finds that the heavier use of the intravenous drugs is not necessarily associated with violent behavior. In his sample the nonassaultives were much heavier users of all drugs, especially marijuana, hashish, the psychedelics and the opiates.

The paranoid thinking generated with amphetamine use is acknowledged by most users, but still often leads to misperception and erroneous interpretations of others' behavior toward the user (Carey and Mandel 1968; Griffith et al. 1972; Kramer, Fischman, and Littlefield 1967). Users have described that during these periods everyone whom they see appears familiar, but other persons' actions appear very aggressive and hostile. Violent paranoid reactions are at times precipitated by seeing the police or persons whom the user misinterprets as narcotic officers. Abusers may become particularly violent when brought to medical institutions and must often be handled with extreme care.

The apparent "hypersexuality" correlated with amphetamine use is discussed in the literature and is reported by the abusers themselves (Carey and Mandel 1968; Bell 1961; Kramer, Fischman, and Littlefield 1967). Various social, interpersonal, intrapsychic, and drug factors are involved. The rush or flash is described as being like a sexual orgasm. This may in part be a result of social definition since there are obvious sexual connotations to all drug use but particularly to intravenous use, expressed in the phrases "shooting (someone) up" or "turning (someone) on." The bend in the arm is referred to as the "cunt" and back and forth drawing of blood into the syringe is referred to as "jacking off." Although physiologically the sympathomimetic qualities of amphetamines inhibit the maintenance of an erection, this same effect tends to facilitate the orgasm, and users report it is of greater intensity and duration and, therefore, more desirable. Sexual activity usually occurs after much of the drug effect has worn off, for users generally report that the flight of ideas accompanying amphetamine intoxication inhibits any sustained concentration upon sexual fantasies or performance. Viva's new book, *Superstar* (1970) describes the milieu and mythology of an amphetamine sexual episode in detail.

Most users report an increase in sexual drives, yet their sexuality tends to be regressed in the form of polymorphous or perverse sexual activity. Auto- or homo-erotic types of sexual activity occur frequently among amphetamine abusers, and genuine heterosexual relationships are rarely sustained (Bell 1961). This may be due to various factors including predisposing personality constellations and social factors, and may be part of the regressive personality factors involved in chronic drug abuse. The compulsiveness of this sexual behavior may be part of the more generalized compulsive behavior (described as stereotyped behavior in animal studies) inherent in amphetamine intoxication (Randrup and Munkvad 1970; Snyder 1972). It may also represent a pathologic search for intimacy in an attempt to fill a void in interpersonal closeness which paradoxically the user's increasing sexual exploits fail to satisfy.

Homosexual or pseudohomosexual panic states (Woods 1972) are occasionally seen particularly among novice users and may reach psychotic proportions. The psychoanalytic literature describes cases of homosexual panic induced by lumbar punctures performed on adolescent males in medical settings, and it is not surprising that, in a setting where a novice is "shot up" by another more experienced user, a homosexual panic reaction may be precipitated.

Prostitutes and hustlers may use the drug to facilitate their activities and to make their actions seem more pleasant. The amphetamines may be used to facilitate other illegal acts, but it must be stressed that many of those who abuse the amphetamines in large amounts are unable to perform illegal acts adequately because of the tremulousness, nervousness, misperception, hypervigilance, and paranoia which they engender (R. C. Smith 1969a and b).

self-medication and progression to other drugs

Subsequent progression to other drugs (e.g., heroin or barbiturates), is often the result of the secondary use of one drug to treat the side effects or withdrawal of another (Langrod 1970; Shick, Smith, and Meyers 1970; Smith, Wesson, and Lannon 1970). Many amphetamine abusers use "downers" like heroin or barbiturates to treat the unpleasant abstinence from amphetamine ("amphetamine blues") or the overstimulation. The acute and chronic abstinence syndrome of the amphetamines is quite unpleasant, and "downers" such as barbiturates and particularly heroin provide a dreamy escape from this overstimulated exhaustion and may themselves become valued for the "high" they produce. This increased use of heroin by amphetamine abusers to treat the undesirable effects of extended amphetamine misuse is another indication of the destructiveness of

amphetamine abuse. The secondary use of such drugs is a phenomenon inherent in the speed scene, as the users attempt to medicate
themselves. The increase in heroin use among the youth of the nation is an alarming phenomenon, and in some communities is related to this progression which appears to predictably follow the
development of a "speed scene" (Shick, Smith, and Meyers 1970).

Patterns of drug use which arise in the Haight or the Bay Area
seem to be repeated after a time lag of a year or so in other urban
drug scenes over the nation, and thus patterns of progression in
the Haight may predict changes which occur elsewhere (Shick,
Smith, and Meyers 1970). During the summer and fall of 1967 a
progression from the exclusive use of marijuana and psychedelics
to the intravenous use of amphetamines began in the Haight. Only
a very small percentage of the "true hippies" who originated the
Haight and who used marijuana socially and LSD in a ritual pattern progressed to amphetamine abuse. The group who rejected
amphetamine and formed a nucleus of "acid heads" left the area
as their life style began to conflict with the increasing numbers of
intravenous abusers (Smith 1969c). There was a group of youthful
habitual psychedelic users in the Haight in 1967 who took LSD
more than three times a week (Schick, Smith, and Meyers 1970;
Shick and Smith 1973) and some of these may have changed their
drug of choice to methamphetamine as it became available. Others
who left the Haight continued to use the psychedelics habitually,
a pattern described in another paper (Shick and Smith 1973).

One explanation advanced for the number of persons turning to
the amphetamines in place of the psychedelics was that during that
summer the influx of the persons into the Haight-Ashbury was so
great that the "confirmed hippies"—who were experienced with
LSD use and who could effectively guide the inexperienced LSD
user—were overwhelmed by the sheer number of persons who were
arriving. They could provide the guidance and setting necessary for
an adequate LSD experience to only a few of the newcomers who
were experimenting with the psychedelics. The extensive use of
LSD in inappropriate settings and uncertain conditions and with
people whom the user might realistically feel he could not trust led
to an increased number of anxiety reactions (bad trips) or merely
unpleasant experiences. Some people continued to use the psychedelics in spite of the occasional unpleasant experiences. This was
reinforced by the ethic that the LSD experience was "good" (i.e.,
desirable), and failure to experience this "good" feeling indicated
unresolved difficulties within the individual. The cure, they said,

was to try again. Many tried LSD again and again, but a number of these persons turned to the use of the amphetamines which tended to relieve anxiety rather than to provoke it. It may be for others that the same underlying personality constellations which caused the bad trips also disposed the individuals to abuse multiple drugs or determined their choice of a peer group who condoned multiple drug use and extensive experimentation.

Furthermore the amphetamines lend themselves more readily to a compulsive pattern of use than do the psychedelics. Since tolerance to the psychedelics develops so rapidly, those persons prone to compulsive patterns of drug use would be expected to turn more frequently to the abuse of the amphetamines than to the psychedelics, even though LSD was the predominant drug of choice at that time (Shick, Smith, and Meyers 1970). The use of LSD and amphetamines together in this setting of indiscriminate use increased the incidence of "bad trips." Many began to use the amphetamines, barbiturates, or heroin to treat the post-LSD depression or "psychedelic confusion" frequently seen after adverse reactions to LSD or habitual psychedelic use (Shick and Freedman 1973). The general knowledge about LSD bad trips and flashbacks, in addition to the controversial chromosome damage, led some experimenters to begin their illicit drug use with the amphetamines in an attempt to avoid difficulties with LSD. "I shot speed first because I was afraid of the bad trips I'd heard about with LSD," said one 19-year-old user.

Presently the speed scene in the Haight has decreased, and the drugs of choice there now are Heroin, barbiturates, and other sedative-hypnotics such as methaqualone and alcohol. The character of the neighborhood has changed as well as the types of people who migrate there. But the decline in the intravenous amphetamine use has been matched by an increased use of speed elsewhere and in diverse population sectors (e.g., high school students), and we believe that heroin and sedative-hypnotic use often follows such speed scenes.

the treatment of amphetamine dependence

Research in nonnarcotic drug abuse is most deficient in the area of treatment, although a few useful articles have appeared (Chambers 1970; Cohen, White, and Schonlar 1971; Tinklenberg 1970; Shick and Freedman 1973). The type of treatment must be individualized to suit the patient—some seem to require hospitalization and others respond to outpatient group or individual psychotherapy. A patient's prognosis seems to depend upon a number of factors including the extent of his present involvement with drugs, the abuse potential of the drugs he presently uses, the total length of time he has used drugs (including alcohol), his present pattern of use and route of administration, the extent of his involvement in a drug-using subculture, his ego strength, object relations, tolerance for frustration, ability to delay gratifications, and a consideration of possible precipitants (Bell 1972). Users who have only an experimental pattern of use of drugs such as psychedelics and amphetamine, who have used drugs only a short time, whose use has begun after adolescence, who are using drugs to solve a life crisis, whose premorbid adjustment has been good, and whose use has been exclusively oral have, in our judgment, the best prognosis.

Usually the experimental *intravenous* amphetamine user is dangerously close to compulsive patterns of drug abuse. Intravenous experience with any drug to any degree often constitutes serious involvement with a drug-abuse scene and implies extensive experience with other drugs. Yet if the intravenous experience is not repeated, it constitutes only experimental use. Experimental drug use may involve the occasional use of an astounding variety of drugs, and the sheer number of drugs used does not provide an adequate estimate of drug-abuse susceptibility.

Severe underlying personality disorganization requires adequate diagnosis and treatment. A number of individuals who have underlying psychiatric disorders—such as manic-depressive psychosis, schizophrenia, organic brain syndrome, sociopathy, or depression—use drugs in an attempt at self-treatment for the symptoms of the underlying disorder.

"Closer scrutiny of the alcoholic (Schuckit et al. 1969; Winokur et al. 1970) has enabled a separation between a primary disorder of alcoholism and alcoholism secondary to an underlining psychiatric illness which predated the onset of alcoholism. Many secondary alcoholic females seem to show a primary affective disorder, developed independently or prior to the abuse of alcohol, and such studies indicate that alcoholism and antisocial behavior are highly correlated, more commonly in men than in women. Similar findings upon closer scrutiny of other forms of serious drug abuse would be anticipated" (Shick and Freedman 1973). Yet it is unclear to what extent treatment of an underlying disorder affects a person's drug use. Occasionally when schizophrenia or manic-depressive disease, for instance, is properly treated with chemotherapy, the patient no longer feels it necessary to continue his drug-abuse habits. On the other hand, if he remains in the drug-abuse scene where his friends continue to use drugs, it is quite difficult for him to remain abstinent even though his underlying difficulties may be adequately managed. Thus, a major part of the treatment of drug abusers is to encourage them to break their former ties with their drug dependent friends, particularly if sustained drug abstinence is the ultimate goal. Certainly one difficulty in the treatment of drug abusers is the lack of adequate facilities for enforcing drug abstinence in a therapeutic setting. "Psychotherapeutic approaches are useful for some drug-using persons and not for others. Difficulty enforcing drug abstinence and the failure to continue contact with a therapist are the most important reasons for disappointing results, and underlying factors are variously understood and communicated by both patient, therapist and researcher. Continuing redefinition, description, and classification of patients and treatments is part of the meaningful categorization aimed toward prediction of who will benefit from psychotherapeutic approaches and exploration of the more subtle variables which lead to improvement or relapse. Inpatient psychiatric facilities are accumulating a vast experience with drug-using adolescents with relatively severe pathology—experience which should generate principles and variables for study. Whether the drugs add anything new to research of delayed development, borderline states, severe character disorders, and schizophrenia prevalent in the 1950s is as yet unclear" (Shick and Freedman 1973). Yet outpatient treatment is not to be disparaged, for often adequate attention to the adverse effects of chronic drug use encourages rapport with a potentially beneficial treatment facility and is a step toward involvement in more efficacious treatment modalities. A large number of drug abusers do not have a disorder which can best be treated simply by chemotherapy, and for these individuals group therapy with other abusers—or in some cases (particularly where only experimental patterns exist)—individual psychotherapy is sometimes successful in encouraging them to give up their drug-abuse habits.

"Since treatment and prevention of nonnarcotic drug abuse is not an advanced art, but rather a tentative, fragmentary and uncertain array of ventures, research is equally relatively undeveloped. Probably—when the novelty dissipates—the same *principles* of diagnosis of situation, person and his dysfunction, the same *resources* that prevail in psychiatric treatments generally, the same *principles* of group, individual, occupational and pharmacotherapeutic treatments, will be applicable" (Shick and Freedman 1973). Occasional relapse into their former drug taking is not necessarily a treatment failure, for drug abuse is a chronic disorder, and during the treatment of any chronic disorder occasional relapses are quite likely to occur. Unfortunately the correct diagnosis is often quite difficult since the psychotic effects and the withdrawal depression which often occur with amphetamine abuse make it difficult to ascertain the underlying personality organization or disorganization of most abusers when they are first seen clinically—or even later, particularly if they continue to use the drugs episodically. As discussed before, it sometimes requires several months of total drug abstinence for the psychotic process or depression induced by the drugs to lift, and initial hospitalization to enforce drug abstinence is often required to separate out those persons with underlying psychopathology amenable to treatment.

Why certain individuals seem to prefer amphetamine to sedative drugs such as barbiturates, alcohol, and heroin remains unexplained, although some reports shed light on the dynamics involved. Whether such drug specificity hypotheses are a major factor is at issue (Wieder and Kaplan 1968; Shick and Freedman 1973). Fischman in a study (1968) comparing heroin addicts to amphetamine addicts, found that preference for stimulants "was determined by the combined influence of cost, legal status of the drug, and their specific type of action . . . [and suggested] that the energizing effect was by far the most important motive for choice." Although understanding the meaning to the patient of different drugs' effects could lead to a deepened understanding of the dynamics of choice and perhaps even quite useful treatment interventions, such differences are often obscured in the present rapidly fluctuating drug-abuse scene where social considerations, drug popularity and fads, and drug use to treat the side effects and withdrawal syndromes of other drugs are often more important determinants of a person's drug choice.

Nowadays rapid fluctuations in popularity of certain drugs of choice make establishment of beneficial programs more difficult. The character of drug abuse in a particular neighborhood often changes almost yearly, and programs must be flexible or they will reach only a particular segment of the drug-abusing population at any one time. No simple solution exists. With the drug problem rapidly increasing in the United States, it is time to emphasize more innovative procedures for treatment and rehabilitation. The classic institutional approach is costly but necessary for some individuals. Those agencies having responsibility for drug-abuse treatment should emphasize flexible community-based programs and should respond quickly to new outbreaks of drug-abuse epidemics within a community (DeAlarcon 1972a; Hughes and Crawford 1972).

There is no simple answer to the problem of amphetamine abuse. Laws need to be changed, but that will not cure the problem. Treatment modalities need to be established, and information disseminated among laymen and physicians alike. People should be informed of the dangers of amphetamines as well as of their potential beneficial effects in hyperkinesis and narcolepsy. Illegal manufacturers and distributors must be reckoned with, and the pharmaceutical industry must realize that it knowingly or unknowingly supplies large quantities of amphetamines and other stimulant drugs which eventually reach illegal channels and are misused.

summary

Amphetamine abuse continues to occur in the United States and is prevalent to an unassessed degree among the youth of the nation and older groups alike. Oral amphetamine abuse among persons who take diet pills and among young users continues for various psychosocial reasons. Abuse of oral preparations is more prevalent than intravenous abuse, which may be a temporary phenomenon. It should be emphasized that alcoholism is America's primary drug-abuse problem, while amphetamine abuse, though on the increase, involves a considerably smaller group of persons. Amphetamine is used in either an experimental, circumstantial-situational or compulsive pattern, and occasionally recreationally. The use of amphetamine in attempts at self-treatment for an underlying disorder or a recent life crisis is recognized. Oral compulsive use is generally of a low-dose maintenance type, while intravenous abuse is presently in high-dose cyclical patterns. The great number of toxic effects described, the high mortality rate, and the rapid progression to other drugs tend to limit the extended abuse of amphetamine intravenously. Persons are often initiated into amphetamine use by friends who offer to "turn them on" or "shoot them up" or by medical personnel (pathologic prescribers) who indiscriminately prescribe the drugs without medical indications. Heroin and barbiturate experimentation is extensive in the speed scene and may be tried initially to counteract the subjective effects of the "crash." Later, heroin may be preferred for its characteristic dreamlike state as an escape from the sufferings of speed abuse. Although the phrase, "speed kills," does not apply to acute effects, deaths from violence, hepatitis, suicide, psychotic behavior, and experimentation with other drugs are daily occurrences. Drug abusers tend to abuse any drug they use, and as the serious consequences of amphetamine abuse become generally known, many multiple drug abusers will choose other drugs. Treatment must be individualized according to various criteria described, but enforced abstinence in a therapeutic hospital setting is often necessary to prevent early relapse during the acute abstinence phase and for the correct diagnosis of the drug-free personality makeup.

REFERENCES

Angrist, B., and Gershon, S. 1970. The phenomenology of experimentally induced amphetamine psychosis: preliminary observations. *Biological Psychiatry* 2:95–107.

————. 1971. *Possible dose response relationships in amphetamine psychosis.* In Press.

Angrist, B., Schweitzer, J., Friedhoff, A. J., Gershon, S., Hekimian, L. J., and Floyd, A. 1969. The clinical symptomatology of amphetamine psychosis and its relationship to amphetamine levels in urine. *International Pharmacopsychiatry* 2:125–39.

Bach-y-rita, G., Lion, J. R., Clement, C. E., and Ervin, F. R. 1971. Episodic dyscontrol: a study of 130 violent patients. *American Journal of Psychiatry* 127:1473–78.

Bejerot, N. 1968. An epidemic of phenmetrazine dependence—epidemiological and clinical aspects. In *The pharmacological and epidemiological aspects of adolescent drug dependence,* ed. C. W. M. Wilson, pp. 55–56. London: Pergamon Press.

Bell, D. S. 1961. Amphetamine addiction and disturbed sexuality. *Archives of General Psychiatry* 4:74–78.

————. 1965. Comparison of amphetamine psychosis and schizophrenia. *British Journal of Psychiatry* 111:701–7.

————. 1972. The precipitants of amphetamine addiction. *British Journal of Psychiatry* 119:171–77.

————, and Trethowan, W. H. 1961. Amphetamine addiction. *Journal of Nervous and Mental Diseases* 133:489–96.

Berg, D. F. 1970. The non-medical use of dangerous drugs in the U.S.: a comprehensive view. *International Journal of the Addictions* 5:777–834.

Blumberg, A. G., Cohen, M., Heaton, A. M., and Klein, D. F. 1971. Covert drug abuse among voluntary hospitalized psychiatric patients. *Journal of the American Medical Association* 217:1659–61.

Bowers, M. B., and Freedman, D. X. 1973. Psychosis associated with drug use. In *American handbook of psychiatry,* vol. 6.

Carey, J. T., and Mandel, J. 1968. A San Francisco Bay Area "speed scene." *Journal of Health and Social Behavior* 9:164–74.

Chambers, C. D. 1970. Some considerations for the treatment of nonnarcotic drug abuses. In *Major modalities in the treatment of drug abuse,* eds. L. Brill and L. Lieberman. Boston: Little, Brown and Company.

Citron, B. P., Halpern, M., McCarron, M., Lundberg, G. D., McCormick, R., Pincus, I. J., Tatter, D., and Haverback, B. J. 1970. Necrotizing angiitis associated with drug abuse. *New England Journal of Medicine* 283:1003–11.

Cohen, C. S., White, E. H., and Schonlar, J. C. 1971. Interpersonal patterns of personality for drug abusing patients and their therapeutic implications. *Archives of General Psychiatry* 24:266–69.

Connell, P. H. 1958. *Amphetamine Psychosis.* London: Mandsley Monographs #5.

———. 1968. Clinical aspects of amphetamine dependence. In *The pharmacological and epidemiological aspects of adolescent drug dependence,* ed. C. W. M. Wilson, pp. 41–53. New York: Pergamon Press.

Cravey, R. H., and Baselt, R. C. 1968. Methamphetamine poisoning. *Journal of the Forensic Science Society* 8:118–20.

DeAlarcon, R. 1972a. Drug abuse as a communicable disease. In *The Milroy lectures.* In Press.

———. 1972b. An epidemiological evaluation of a public health measure aimed at reducing the availability of methamphetamine. *Psychological Medicine* 2:293–300.

Eisenberg, L. 1971. Principles of drug therapy in child psychiatry with special reference to stimulant drugs. *American Journal of Orthopsychiatry* 41:371–79.

———. 1972. The hyperkinetic child and stimulant drugs. *New England Journal of Medicine* 287:249–50.

Ellinwood, E. H. 1967. Amphetamine psychosis: 1. Description of the individuals and process. *Journal of Nervous and Mental Diseases* 144:273–83.

———. 1968. Amphetamine psychosis: 2. Theoretical implications. *International Journal of Neuropsychiatry* 4:45–54.

———. 1971. Assault and homicide associated with amphetamine abuse. *American Journal of Psychiatry* 127:1170–75.

Espelin, D. E., and Done, A. K. 1969. Amphetamine poisoning: effectiveness of chlorpromazine. *New England Journal of Medicine* 278:1361–65.

Fischer, C. M., Smith, D. E., Schonfeld, E., and Hine, C. H. 1969. Behavioral mediators in the polyphasic mortality curve of aggregate amphetamine toxicity. *Journal of Psychedelic Drugs* 2:55–84.

Fischmann, M. W. and Schuster, C. R. 1973. Behavioral toxicity of chronic methamphetamine in the Rhesus Monkey. In *Behavioral toxicology,* eds. B. Weiss and V. Laties. New York: Appleton-Century-Crofts.

Fischman, V. S. 1968. Stimulant users in the California Rehabilitation Center. *International Journal of the Addictions* 3:113–30.

Fish, B. 1971. The "one child, one drug" myth of stimulants in hyperkinesis. *Archives of General Psychiatry* 25:193–203.

Freedman, D. X. 1970. Amphetamine and cocaine abuse: letters to the editor. *Postgraduate Medicine* 47:57–59.

――――. 1971. Report of the conference on the use of stimulant drugs in the treatment of behaviorally disturbed young school children. Office of Child Development, Department of Health, Education, and Welfare, Washington, D.C.

Freud, S. 1963. *The Cocaine Papers.* Vienna: Duquin Press.

Gay, G. R., Winkler, J. J., and Newmeyer, J. A. 1971. Emerging trends of heroin abuse in the San Francisco Bay Area. *Journal of Psychedelic Drugs* 4:53–64.

Goodman, L. S., and Gilman, A. 1970. *The Pharmacologic Basis of Therapeutics.* New York: The Macmillan Company.

Goodwin, D. W., Alderson, P., and Rosenthal, R. 1971. Clinical significance of hallucinations in psychiatric disorders. *Archives of General Psychiatry* 24:76–80.

Gottschalk, L. A., Bates, D. E., Fox, R. A., and James, J. M. 1971. Psychoactive drug use. *Archives of General Psychiatry* 25:395–97.

Griffith, J. D. 1966. A study of illicit amphetamine drug traffic in Oklahoma City. *American Journal of Psychiatry* 123:560–69.

――――, Cavenaugh, J., Held, J., and Oates, J. A. 1972. Dextroamphetamine: evaluation of psychotomimetic properties in man. *Archives of General Psychiatry* 26:97–100.

Griffith, J. D., Davis, J., and Oates, J. 1971. Amphetamines: addiction to a nonaddicting drug. In *Advances in Neuropsychopharmacology,* eds. O. Vinar et al. Amsterdam: North Holland Publishing Company.

Hawks, D., Micheson, M., Ogborne, A., and Edwards, G. 1969. The abuse of methylamphetamine. *British Medical Journal* 2:715–21.

Hofer, R. and Pittel, S. M. 1971. Characteristics of amphetamine use in a hippie subculture. Presented at American Psychological Association annual meeting, September 4, 1971.

Horowitz, M. J. 1969. Flashbacks: recurrent intrusive images after the use of LSD. *American Journal of Psychiatry* 126:565–69.

Howard, J., and Borges, P. 1971. Needle sharing in the Haight: some social and psychological functions. *Journal of Psychedelic Drugs* 4:71–80.

Hughes, P. H. and Crawford, G. A. 1972. A contagious disease model for researching and interviewing in heroin epidemics. *Archives of General Psychiatry* 27:149–55.

Hughes, P. H., and Jaffe, J. H. 1971. Heroin epidemics in Chicago. In *Proceedings of the fifth world congress of psychiatry.*

Jones, E. 1953. *The life and work of Sigmund Freud,* vol. 1. New York: Basic Books, Inc.

Jonsson, L. E., and Gunne, L. M. 1970. Clinical studies of amphetamine psychosis. In *Amphetamine and related compounds,* eds. E. Costa and S. Garattini, pp. 929–36. New York: Raven Press.

Kornetsky, C. 1970. Psychoactive drugs in the immature organism. *Psychopharmacologia* 17:105–36.

Kosman, M. E., and Unna, K. R. 1968. The effects of chronic administration of the amphetamine and other stimulants on behavior. *Clinical Pharmacology and Therapeutics* 9:240–54.

Kramer, J. C., Fischman, V. S., and Littlefield, D. C. 1967. Amphetamine abuse. *Journal of the American Medical Association* 201:305–09.

Langrod, J. 1970. *Secondary drug use among heroin users.* In Press.

Louria, D. B., Hensle, T., and Rose, J. 1967. The major medical complications of heroin addiction. *Annals of Internal Medicine* 67:1–22.

Martin, W. R., Sloan, J. W., Sapira, J. D., and Jadinski, D. R. 1971. Physiologic, subjective, and behavioral effects of amphetamine, methamphetamine, ephedrine, phenmetrazine, and methylphenidate in man. *Clinical Pharmacology and Therapeutics* 12:245–58.

Mellinger, G. D., Balter, M. B., and Manheimer, D. I. 1971. Patterns of psychotherapeutic drug use among adults in San Francisco. *Archives of General Psychiatry* 25:385–94.

Mendelson, W., Johnson, N., and Stewart, M. A. 1971. Hyperactive children as teenagers: a following study. *Journal of Nervous and Mental Diseases* 153:273–79.

Menkes, M. M., Rowe, J. S., and Menkes, J. H. 1967. A twenty-five year followup study of the hyperkinetic child with minimal brain dysfunction. *Pediatrics* 39:393–99.

Meyers, F. N., Jawetz, E., and Goldfien, A. 1968. *A review of medical pharmacology.* Los Altos, California: Lange Medical Publications, pp. 46–59.

National Commission on Marihuana and Drug Abuse. 1972. *Drug Use in America: Problem in Perspective.* Second report, Washington: U.S. Government Printing Office.

Oswald, I., and Thacore, U. R. 1963. Amphetamine and phenmetrazine addiction physiological abnormalities in the abstinence syndrome. *British Medical Journal* 427:31.

Parry, H. J., Balter, M. B., Mellinger, G. D., Cisin, I. H., and Manheimer, D. I. 1973. National patterns of psychotherapeutic drug use. *Archives of General Psychiatry* 28:769–83.

Pittel, S. and Hofer, R. 1970. The transition to amphetamine abuse. Unpublished manuscript.

Randrup, A., and Munkvad, I. 1970. Biochemical, anatomical and psychological investigations of stereotyped behavior induced by amphetamines. In *Amphetamine and related compounds,* eds. E. Costa and S. Garattini, pp. 695–714. New York: Raven Press.

Robbins, E. S., Robbins, L., Frosch, W. A., and Stern, M. 1968. College student drug use. *American Journal of Psychiatry* 126:1743–51.

Rockwell, E. A., and Ostwalt, P. 1968. Amphetamine use and abuse in psychiatric patients. *Archives of General Psychiatry* 18:612–16.

Rumbaugh, C., Bergeron, R. T., Fang, H. C. H., and McCormick, R. 1971. Cerebral angiographic changes in the drug abuse patient. *Radiology* 101:335–44.

Rumbaugh, C., Bergeron, R. T., Scanlon, R. L., Teal, J. S., Segall, H. D., Fang, H. C. H., and McCormick, R. 1971. Cerebral vascular changes secondary to amphetamine abuse in the experimental animal. *Radiology* 101:345–51.

Schuckit, M., Pitts, F. N., Jr., Reich, T., King, L. J., and Winokur, G. 1969. Alcoholism 1. Two types of alcoholism in women. *Archives of General Psychiatry* 20:301–06.

Scott, P. D., and Buckell, M. 1971. Delinquency and amphetamines. *British Journal of Psychiatry* 119:179–82.

Shick, J. F. E., and Freedman, D. X. 1973. Research in nonnarcotic drug abuse. *American Handbook of Psychiatry*, vol. 6. In Press.

Shick, J. F. E., and Smith, D. E. 1970. Analysis of the LSD flashback. *Journal of Psychedelic Drugs* 3:13–19.

———. 1973. The illicit use of the psychotomimetic amphetamines with special reference to STP (DOM) toxicity. *Journal of Psychedelic Drugs*. In Press.

———, and Meyers, F. H. 1970. Patterns of drug use in the Haight-Ashbury neighborhood. *Clinical Toxicology* 3:19–56.

Smith, D. E. 1969a. The characteristics of dependence in high-dose methamphetamine abuse. *International Journal of Addictions* 4:453–459.

———. 1969b. Physical vs. psychological dependence and tolerance in high-dose methamphetamine abuse. *Clinical Toxicology* 2:99–103.

———. 1969c. Speed freaks vs. acid heads: conflict between drug subcultures. *Clinical Pediatrics* 8:185–92.

———. 1970. *The new social drug.* Englewood Cliffs, N. J.: Prentice-Hall, Inc.

———, and Fischer, C. M. 1969. Acute amphetamine toxicity. *Journal of Psychedelic Drugs* 2:47–53.

———. 1970. An analysis of 310 cases of acute high-dose methamphetamine toxicity in Haight-Ashbury. *Clinical Toxicology* 3:117–24.

Smith, R. C. 1969a. Traffic in amphetamines: patterns of illegal manufacture and distribution. *Journal of Psychedelic Drugs* 2:27–37.

———. 1969b. The world of the Haight-Ashbury speed freak. *Journal of Psychedelic Drugs* 2:186–195.

Snyder, S. H. 1972. Catecholamines in the brain as mediators of amphetamine psychosis. *Archives of General Psychiatry* 27:169–79.

———, Taylor, K. M., Coyle, J. T., and Meyerhoff, J. L. 1970. The role of brain dopamine in behavioral relation and the actions of psychotropic drugs. *American Journal of Psychiatry* 127:199–207.

Tinklenberg, J. 1970. A current view of the amphetamines. Presented at the Western Institute of Drug Problems, Portland State University, Portland, Oregon, August 1970.

———. 1972. Drugs and crime: a consultant's report. Prepared for the National Commission on Marihuana and Drug Abuse.

———, and Woodrow, K. M. 1973. Drug use among youthful assaultive and sexual offenders. In *Aggression: Proceedings of the 1972 annual meet-*

ing of the *Association for Research in Nervous and Mental Disease,* ed. S. H. Frazier. Baltimore: Williams and Wilkins Co.

Utena, H. 1966. Behavioral abberations in methamphetamine-intoxicated animals and chemical correlates in the brain. In *Progress in brain research,* eds. T. Tokizane and J. P. Schade, vol. 21B, pp. 192–207. New York: American Elsevier Publishing Co.

Viva. 1970. *Superstar* pp. 225–59. New York: G. P. Putnam's Sons.

Weiss, G., Minde, K., Werry, J. S., Douglas, V. and Nemeth, E. 1971. Studies on the hyperactive child VIII. Five year follow-up. *Archives of General Psychiatry* 24:409–14.

Weiss, S. R., Raskino, R., Morganstern, N. L. 1970 Intracerebral and subarachnoid hemorrhage following use of methamphetamine. *International Surgery* 53:123–27.

Weissman, A. 1968. Psychopharmacological effects of thiothixene and related compounds. *Psychopharmacologia* 12:142–57.

Wieder, H. and Kaplan, E. H. 1969. Drug use in adolescents—psychodynamic meaning and pharmacogenic effect. *The Psychoanalytic Study of the Child* 24:389–431.

Winokur, G., Reich, T., Rimmer, J. and Pitts, F. N. 1970. Alcoholism III. diagnosis and familial psychotic illness in 259 alcoholic probands. *Archives of General Psychiatry* 23:104–11.

Woods, S. M. 1972. Violence: psychotherapy of pseudohomosexual panic. *Archives of General Psychiatry* 27:255–58.

Zaks, M. S., Hughes, P., Jaffe, J., and Dolkart, M. B. 1969. *Young people in the park.* Presented at American Orthopsychiatric Association Annual Meeting.

Zalis, E. G., Lundberg, G. E., and Knutson, R. A. 1967. The pathophysiology of acute amphetamine poisoning with pathological correlations. *Journal of Pharmacology and Experimental Therapeutics* 158:115–27.

the transition to amphetamine abuse[†]

Stephen M. Pittel / Ricardo Hofer

The growing problem of amphetamine abuse by American youth is currently pre-empting much of the concern previously focused on the use of psychedelic drugs. In an effort to understand the increased use of amphetamines in the drug culture, we have studied a group of young drug users who have made a transition from the predominant use of psychedelics to the predominant use of amphetamines, or who use both drugs concurrently. Examination of some of the psychological factors underlying the choice of drugs among these subjects suggests a number of hypotheses which can help us to understand the increased use of amphetamines in the general culture.

In the early days of the hippie movement in the Haight-Ashbury neighborhood of San Francisco, most of the hippies had a strong antipathy toward "speed freaks," and warnings that "speed kills" were widely circulated. Amphetamine users coexisted with the "flower children" of 1967, but there is some evidence to suggest that few of the original hippies were using amphetamines at that time. Dealers of psychedelic drugs and marijuana rarely catered to the needs of the amphetamine users, and "speed freaks" were generally distrusted and isolated from the rest of the community. (Pittel 1968; Von Hoffman 1968).[*] A statement made by Allen Ginsberg to an

[†] An earlier version of this paper was presented at the Duke University Medical School conference on Current Concepts on Amphetamine Abuse, June 1970 and was previously published in E. Ellinwood and S. Cohen (eds.) *Current Concepts on Amphetamine Abuse*. Washington, D.C.: U.S. Government Printing Office, 1972 (DHEW Publication No. HSM 72–9085).

The research reported herein was supported by National Institute of Mental Health grant number ROI MH-15737.

[*] This statement is supported by the relatively small number of amphetamine users treated at the Haight-Ashbury Free Medical Clinic during the spring and summer of 1967. While approximately 75 per cent of the adverse drug reactions

underground newspaper (*The Electric Newspaper* of Salt Lake City, Utah) typified the attitudes of the hippie community toward amphetamine users:

> Let's issue a general declaration to all the underground community *contra speed-amos ex cathedra*. Speed is anti-social, paranoid making, it's a drag, bad for your body, bad for your mind, generally speaking, in the long run uncreative and it's a plague in the whole dope industry. All the nice gentle dope fiends are getting screwed up by the real horror monster Frankenstein speed-freaks who are going around stealing and bad-mouthing everybody. (Wiener 1969).

Despite such warnings from sources assumed to be acceptable to the authority-wary hippies, it is now commonly believed that amphetamines are more prevalent than psychedelics in the Haight-Ashbury neighborhood and in other hippie enclaves throughout the country.

intruders in the counter-culture

To explain the cultural transition from the use of psychedelics to the use of amphetamines, some observers (Shick, Smith, and Meyers 1969; Smith, Luce, and Dernburg 1970) argue that the real hippies ("the nice gentle dope fiends") emigrated from the Haight-Ashbury as a result of increasing difficulties in making their Utopian experiment work, and they were replaced by a large group of less idealistic types, who used amphetamines and other "hard" drugs. In contrast to the use of psychedelics, said to be motivated by a quest for increased awareness and spiritual development, the use of amphetamines is attributed to the severe psychopathology and generalized deviance thought to be characteristic of these intruders in the counter-culture. Amphetamine use is frequently cited as the explanation for the increased violence and criminality in the Haight-Ashbury neighborhood, and many young people place the responsibility for adverse reactions to psychedelic drugs on the amphetamines with which they allegedly are combined or adulterated. (Shick, Smith, and Meyers 1969).

---

treated at this clinic were related to psychedelics, a similar proportion of patients treated at the San Francisco General Hospital during the same period were amphetamine users. (*1*)

The authors would like to acknowledge their debt to Victor Calef, M.D., Roy Gryler, M.D., Linda Hilles, M.D., Phyllis Kempner, Ph.D., and Robert Wallerstein, M.D., for their contributions to the ideas presented in this paper. We would also like to thank Richard Kendall and Amira Wallach for their assistance in the collection and analysis of data.

To support the view that the cultural transition to amphetamine use is based on the emergence of a new population of drug users who have little in common with the hippies, attention has been focused on the many contrasting effects of amphetamines and psychedelics, and on the radical difference between the life style of the hippies and that of amphetamine abusers. The emphasis on the *differences* among drug users is espoused by two disparate groups. On the one hand are the apologists who attempt to maintain a praiseworthy image of the hippies and of psychedelic drugs by attributing the social degeneration and psychiatric casualties of the current Haight-Ashbury scene to the intentional or inadvertent use of amphetamines. On the other hand are those who believe that individuals have unique predispositions to the use of one or another type of drug. (Hartmann 1969; Frosch 1970; Wieder and Kaplan 1969). According to this theory, the effects of each type of drug fulfill specific and long-standing needs of the user. Both of these groups would expect to find great differences in background or in personality organization between users of the two types of drugs.

Little objective evidence is available to test these assumptions about the reasons for the transition to amphetamine use in the hippie culture. It is quite clear that the modal patterns of drug use, life style, and community involvement in the Haight-Ashbury neighborhood have changed considerably in the past few years. To attribute these changes, however, simply to the influx of a totally different type of person or to the effects of a totally different type of drug precludes any analysis of the complex interactions among personal, social, and pharmacological variables. We also believe it would be a grave error to overlook the growing problem of amphetamine abuse among those who were once committed to the hippie culture and to the use of psychedelic drugs.[1]

the haight-ashbury research project

The amphetamine-using subjects described in this paper were drawn from a larger group of young drug users who have been studied intensively as part of a longitudinal investigation based in the Haight-Ashbury neighborhood of San Francisco. Each partici-

[1] There is some evidence to suggest that many of the current residents of Haight-Ashbury are quite similar in background and in personality organization to the early hippies (Kendall and Pittel 1971) and that many of those currently using amphetamines might have chosen different patterns of drug use had they entered the hippie community a few years earlier (R. C. Smith 1969).

pant in this research is assessed initially through a battery of tests, interviews, questionnaires, and self-descriptions designed to obtain information about his background, attitudes, current functioning, drug use, and involvement in the drug culture. Through whatever factors determine the self-selection of volunteer subjects for this research, we have found that this group of approximately 250 subjects appears to be more representative of the stereotype of early hippies, or flower children, than of the "street people" who are now thought to dominate the neighborhood (Kendall and Pittel 1970). The majority of them come from middle- and upper-middle-class backgrounds and have had at least one or two years of college education; virtually all of them espouse the values which we associate with the hippie ethos. A number of these subjects were among the early hippie residents of Haight-Ashbury, and many of them have been involved in the drug culture since its beginnings a few years ago.

From their varied and extensive histories of drug use, we have classified the majority of our subjects as multiple users. Despite their tendency to experiment with a great number of drugs and for some to indulge in episodic shifts in their primary drug of choice, almost all of our subjects show a decided preference for the use of psychedelic drugs and marijuana. Many of them use amphetamines, barbiturates, and narcotics concurrently with psychedelics, but relatively few are heavily committed to the use of these other drugs.[2]

some similarities between amphetamine and psychedelic drug users

On the surface, the amphetamine users in our sample do not appear to differ significantly from those who use only psychedelic drugs. They come from similar backgrounds, espouse similar values, and manifest many of the same impairments in ego-functioning which we have found in users of psychedelic drugs. (Calef et al. 1970). While there is some tendency for them to be rated as having more severe psychopathology than is characteristic of the total sample, this difference is slight and may be partially or largely accounted for

[2] Among those subjects who do use amphetamines, either concurrently with psychedelics or as their primary drug of choice, there are few who would be classified as particularly heavy users. Even those who use amphetamines intravenously do not tend to show the extreme patterns of high-dose amphetamine abuse described in the recent literature (R. C. Smith 1969; D. E. Smith 1969). The high-dose abuser of amphetamines is probably too hyperactive, suspicious, and fearful to volunteer as a research subject.

by the bias introduced through knowledge of their amphetamine use.

The finding that amphetamine users among our hippie subjects do not seem appreciably different from psychedelic users in terms of background, values, and life style is in itself an argument against the notion that the cultural increase in amphetamine use is due simply to the influx of a totally different kind of user.* We shall turn now to a discussion of some of the psychological factors which led to a transition from psychedelic drugs to amphetamines among our sample of hippie subjects.

the subjective effects of psychedelic drugs

One striking difference between amphetamine and psychedelic drugs which emerges from our data is the quality of subjects' reports of their drug experiences. Subjects describing their use of psychedelics tend to give detailed accounts of rich perceptual and cognitive experiences. These descriptions are quite similar to those reported in the literature (Kluver 1966; Masters and Houston 1966; Metzner 1968), and they are frequently presented as having had profound religious or philosophical impact. The following fragment from a first psychedelic experience was presented by a 21-year-old girl as a major factor in her decision to enter the hippie culture:

> I hadn't wanted to take it [mescaline] but R had a way of imposing his quite strong will on others, and since I loved him and wanted to do what he wanted, I took it—two medium large capsules of white powder. He also took two caps—then his friends came to pick us up in their used ambulance. We went up to Mt. Tamalpais for a rock-music happening in the mountain theater there. I had just begun to come on to it by the time we got there, but as the day progressed, I discovered many new and beautiful things happening. The first thing I noticed was the abundance of gorgeous *colors* around me. Everything was *so colorful!* Some boy had jars of fluorescent paint and brushes and I painted my hands and face with them. I was so enthralled by the liquid beauty of the paints that I went around to all the other people I could reach and put spots of paint on their hands very slowly and carefully, explaining to them as I did that the universe was in those colors and that I was giving them a part of myself at the same time. R and I sat together . . . and pressed our fingers

---

* As has been noted previously, high-dose amphetamine users are not well represented in our sample and may not be amenable to the rigorous assessment procedures we employ. It is not certain how they might compare with either amphetamine or psychedelic users who voluntarily participate in such research.

to our eyes—we could see whole scenes behind our eyelids—bright yellow-green people and things with glowing magenta outlines. Not just anything, either! We both saw the same things, and told each other what we saw. . . . While we were there, a parachutist jumped from a plane and landed in the center of the amphitheater. Everyone but me moved away from the spot he was going to land in. I had never seen a jump and couldn't move from the spot. When he landed about ten feet in front of me, the parachute of orange and white silk settled down on top of me. It was the most beautiful, religious thing that ever happened to me. . . . [later] I began to hallucinate heavily for the first time. I was sitting on a Persian rug and pictures like cartoons began to move on it. I watched a Mickey Mouse and Goofy cartoon in the center, then watched ducks swimming around the edge of the rug turn into long-haired maidens swimming together with graceful strokes. Tactile hallucinations also occurred—my hair and scalp became elastic—I could stretch it across the room and let it snap back. I felt my cheeks disappear and cold air blow through from one side of my face to the other. I also saw inside of my mind as a dark, lonely, cobwebbed cave, with two windows with the shades pulled down as my eyes.

This description illustrates a number of the perceptual and cognitive phenomena which characterize the psychedelic experience and which are valued and sought by users of these drugs. Included here, to varying degrees, are reports of enhanced awareness and perceptual acuity; feelings of closeness, sharing, and ability to communicate; a sense of brotherhood and unity; religious ecstasy; and a variety of perceptual anomalies which are the source of amusement, pleasure, and "insights" into the nature of the self and the world. Other common phenomena not included in this example may be seen as variations of the same themes, all of which suggest that the psychedelic experience is typically one of great beauty, tranquility, and inner harmony.[3]

The passivity of the psychedelic experience is one of its most important, yet often overlooked, characteristics. Even when other people are present during a "trip," the psychedelic user is rarely involved with them actively, and many users describe the necessity of overcoming the desire to seek stimulation or interaction with others as a prerequisite to having a good experience. Given the regressive nature of the psychedelic experience, presumably elicited by drug-induced perceptual distortions (Pittel 1969) it is not surprising that users have little volitional control over their responses (Kluver 1966). Further, the user must be capable of tolerating this

[3] This description does not apply, obviously, to adverse psychedelic experiences ("bad trips"), which are characterized in almost opposite terms.

regressive experience without fearing loss of control. Adverse psychedelic reactions are frequently associated with futile attempts to
alter the nature of the "trip" through directed activity or by efforts
to fight against an impending alteration in consciousness. In some
cases, adverse reactions appear to be precipitated by the user's inability to respond to an actual situational demand while in the
drug-induced state. What seems clear in each of these cases is that
passivity and the ability to relinquish control are essential to the
psychedelic experience and that the inability to remain passive may
lead to significantly different, and often unpleasant experiences.

the subjective effects of amphetamines

In sharp contrast to descriptions of psychedelic experiences, accounts of amphetamine experiences make little mention of the subjective effects of these drugs; rather, they tend to focus on the typically frenetic activities of the user while he is under the influence
of the drug. References to conscious experience are limited typically to mention of an increased rate of mental activity, hypersensi-
tivity to environmental stimulation, increased feelings of strength
and competence, and feelings of euphoria and exhilaration. The following abstracts from subjects' accounts illustrate these themes:

> On speed I became free of inhibitions—had a surplus of energy and
> found I enjoyed having six million thoughts going through my head
> at once. . . .

> The first time I took some amphetamines, I liked it a lot. I was
> very energetic, my thought patterns were faster, and I felt that my
> memory power was increased. None of the nervousness that I had
> expected came about . . .

> First time I shot speed . . . can dig the needle shooting up trip
> . . . You just feel straight energy-power-good feeling. Then you feel
> super together and excited and intelligent and clear and rap and rap
> and your head may be together but you lose contact with reality—I'm
> not here, but like later when you start crashing you can see all the
> delusions you were under.

> . . . I invited a boy over whom I had just met in the street . . .
> and we dropped some speed. I remember feeling intensely happy and
> satisfied—"together" with myself. I told him things about myself I
> would never have told anyone—he did the same. We felt the same,
> almost as one. It seemed that all my life I had worked to feel as I
> did on speed. It was wonderful to know that I had finally reached
> my goal.

. . . two years on speed—diet pills and shots of amphetamines mixed with vitamins. I was extremely nervous, emotional, speeded, fragmented, could do no work efficiently but felt generally manic. For some reason I did not relate my frequent crashes to the speed—I was too delighted with the energy it gave me.

The poverty of these descriptions is particularly noteworthy in the light of Ellinwood's findings (1967) that amphetamine users are capable of almost total recall of their drug experiences. If we assume that our subjects selectively recall (or choose to recount) those drug experiences which strike them as most profound and which are most highly valued, amphetamine use would seem to be based primarily on its effects on mood and behavior. Alterations in the *content* of perceptions and ideation are reported occasionally, but these are insignificant in comparison to more universal affective changes and the elevation of self-esteem and confidence.[4]

In addition to their energizing and antidepressant effects, the amphetamines also produce a variety of somatic experiences which are of great importance in distinguishing their effects from those of psychedelic drugs. Somatic reactions to psychedelic drugs tend to occur, if at all, early in the experience; they usually disappear before the onset of the perceptual phenomena which mark the beginning of the "trip." (Hollister 1968). These reactions, which might include nausea, dizziness, tremors, and feelings of weakness, are all experienced as unpleasant and are seen invariably as side-effects independent of the psychedelic experience itself. With amphetamines, however, the relationship between somatic and psychic phenomena is entirely different. Those who take high doses of the drugs place particular emphasis on the intensely pleasurable experience of the "flash" or "rush" which quickly follows injection of the drug; for some users, this orgasmic experience may be the primary motive for high-dose abuse. (Carey and Mandel 1968). More moderate users do not report these intense experiences, but there are almost universal reports of long-lasting visceral and peripheral effects resulting from the parasympathomimetic action of the drug.

These effects, coupled with the increased tendency toward restlessness and the need to be active, contribute greatly to the amphetamine user's awareness of himself as an entity separate from his sur-

---

[4] The significance of perceptual and ideational effects in amphetamine abuse may be somewhat exaggerated in the literature dealing with high-dosage abusers suffering from toxic psychoses. Phenomenological reports drawn from patients with amphetamine psychoses contain a number of elements (including auditory and visual hallucinations) not seen typically in more moderate users (Ellinwood 1967; Angrist and Gershon 1969).

roundings. In contrast to psychedelic drugs, which often lead to experiences of loss of body boundaries, fusion, and "ego dissolution," amphetamines lead to a sharper definition of the body image. (Adler 1970). For males, the combination of the energizing and somatic effects seems to enhance the sense of masculinity, and perhaps the sexual drive. The passive receptive experience associated with psychedelic use, on the other hand, is most often described as having strong feminine characteristics.

We could give many other illustrations of the antithetical effects of amphetamines and psychedelic drugs—for example, the aggressiveness and hostility seen among amphetamine users and the pacifism and denial of hostility characteristic of psychedelic users. Most of these additional examples, however, would only reinforce the concept that these drugs give rise to widely disparate somatic, subjective, and behavioral effects, virtually all of which can be shown to relate to the differences already noted.

the transition from psychedelics to amphetamines: hypotheses

In view of these contrasting characteristics of psychedelic and amphetamine effects, how do we account for the fact that many individuals use these drugs concurrently, and for the transition from psychedelic drugs to amphetamines? Two hypotheses will be considered here.

failure of psychedelic drugs to compensate for impairments in ego-functioning

In previous papers (Calef et al. 1970; Pittel 1969) we have attempted to show that our subjects use psychedelic drugs to compensate for certain long-standing impairments in ego-functioning. As one example of such impairment, we have described the typical failure of our subjects in integrating and synthesizing experience—an impairment which has profound consequences on virtually all aspects of their functioning. By providing them with an experience characterized by a great sense of harmony or by helping them externalize their inner fragmentation and disorganization, psychedelic drugs bring about a temporary reduction in their chronic anxiety and renewed faith in their ability to deal with personal and social problems.[5] Many of them believe that psychedelic drugs will provide

---

[5] Thus, the frequent claim of our subjects that their use of psychedelic drugs is motivated by and results in self-cure.

them with the key to better understanding of themselves and of their environment.

From the standpoint of an outside observer, these beliefs about their increased capacity to integrate experience and to cope with problems are illusory, if not delusional. Our data suggest that psychedelic drug experiences lead to further impairment of ego functions and to an even greater inability to resolve psychological problems. In addition, users must eventually face their disenchantment with a drug that they invested with the powers of a panacea. It is at this point that the transition to amphetamines may occur.

The typical rationalization for this transition is that amphetamines provide needed energy and motivation for constructive promlem solving. The user feels that, through his use of amphetamines, he is overcoming the passivity associated with psychedelic drugs. Viewing these subjects psychologically, one can discern an attempt to strengthen ego boundaries and to shore up whatever reality-testing ability and synthesizing capacity they may retain. Other desired effects of amphetamines are their ability to counteract increasing anxiety and depression and the sense of pervasive emptiness that results from continued failure to deal with persisting or exacerbated personal problems.

adverse and idiosyncratic experiences with psychedelic drugs

The foregoing hypothesis does not account for the transition from psychedelics to amphetamines in all cases. There exists a second group of subjects whose psychedelic experiences were not conducive to the ideological commitment described above. Included in this second group are: 1) those whose experiences with psychedelics were predominantly adverse; 2) those who failed to achieve *any* psychedelic effect; and 3) those whose psychedelic experiences are highly idiosyncratic, being more amphetamine-like than psychedelic in quality.

The psychedelic experiences of subjects who fall into this category are typically lacking in rich descriptive detail. In describing them, these subjects tend to focus primarily on the circumstances and setting of the "trip," on unpleasant somatic effects, and on their behavior rather than on their inner experiences. Few of the perceptual, cognitive, or metaphysical phenomena described by subjects who become committed to the use of psychedelic drugs are found in the protocols of this group of subjects. The following excerpts are taken from descriptions of the first psychedelic experiences of subjects who later shifted to amphetamines:

> . . . I bought my first cap of acid from a friend. I took it at home on a Friday night before supper. I started getting high while I was eating, and my food started moving around on my plate. Also, I kept smiling and grinning. I noticed a lot of body feelings, twitches and tingling all over. Then I went in to watch TV and I began to feel warm, good sensations all over, and the TV began to melt and the actors' words were noticeably distorted. I went into my room and hallucinated insects crawling on the ceiling while I was listening to records. My sister came in with a bowl of potato chips and I ate some and freaked 'cause it tasted like glass crunched up. Then I listened to music for about four hours and dozed off.

> I was on liberty from my ship in the Navy. I was visiting friends in the Haight. A friend of one of my friends turned us on to a tab of "blue cheer" each. I dropped it and we went to a concert at Speed-way Meadows because it was Sunday. Just before we got there I began to feel very light. The music manifested itself in visions of lightning. After awhile I decided to come back up Haight Street. The air in the park was white with yellow spots. I hallucinated in a screen effect with the background looking normal, but at times the background looked like a photographic negative or as through a red or blue filter. Sensually I felt good all over. On Haight Street, I went down shaking everybody's hand, saying "Hello, brother, sister." I was very conscious of love. I could feel, see, and hear its manifestations quite clearly.

In both of these examples there are indications that the drug had some psychedelic effects. Perceptual distortions, somatic changes, and even hallucinatory experiences were reported by both subjects. What is lacking in these descriptions is any symbolic elaboration or generalization of these effects which gives them a special significance. Unlike the experiences reported by subjects who remain committed to psychedelics, these descriptions do not go far beyond a mere cataloging of effects. Neither of the subjects reported the profoundly moving sense of harmony or inner peace which is characteristic of more representative psychedelic experiences. Also, these examples place considerably more emphasis on somatic effects and on activity than is found in most of our data, suggesting that subjects of this type cannot give themselves up to the passivity or to the diffusion of body image which normally occurs with psychedelic drug use.

Psychedelic drugs may be used by these subjects as a means of establishing relationships within the hippie culture or in response to peer pressures. In some cases the use of psychedelics is continued, despite the failure to experience their full effects, or after repeated adverse experiences, because the subjects feel they can overcome their inhibitions and "hang-ups" through mastery of the psychedelic experience.[6]

It can be hypothesized that this group of subjects, although they are motivated to seek the reputed benefits of psychedelic drugs, lack the ability to tolerate the passive and regressive aspects of the psychedelic experience. This inability may be due to an already excessive degree of ego disorganization, or to a rigid and brittle defensive structure which does not allow for regressive experiences. In either case, the anxiety produced by psychedelic drugs can be observed or inferred from their descriptions of such experiences. The transition to amphetamine use by these subjects may be seen as an attempt to strengthen their already shaky ability to maintain control and to compensate for basic impairments in ego functions.

conclusion

In this chapter, we have presented observations and hypotheses bearing upon the use of amphetamines among a group of hippie subjects. We have suggested that an understanding of the motives and personality characteristics underlying the transition from psychedelic drugs to amphetamines is important to any consideration of the cultural changes in patterns of drug abuse. An analysis of our subjects' phenomenological descriptions of their amphetamine and psychedelic experiences suggests that those subjects who make a transition to the concomitant or predominant use of amphetamines do so either because of the increased anxiety and lack of motivation related to their use of psychedelics or because of personality characteristics which make the use of psychedelics intolerable to them.

[6] Among this group of former psychedelic users who have made a transition to the use of amphetamines are a number of subjects whose use of psychedelics was unusually great for a relatively brief span. It is possible that these subjects, one of whom claims to have taken one to three LSD "trips" daily for a six-month period, quickly develop tolerance for the drug. In this way, they are able to avoid experiences which they could not otherwise tolerate, and at the same time remain *bona fide* members of the drug culture.

These subjects may also turn to the use of barbiturates, narcotics, or other psychotropic drugs in their search for an altered state of consciousness that they can tolerate. In subsequent papers, we will attempt to show that the ultimate choice of a drug can be predicted from the nature of the user's initial response to psychedelic drugs.

REFERENCES

Adler, M. 1970. Drug abuse as the manipulation of body image, sensibility, and self: the antinomian personality as tuned organism. Paper presented at the Conference on Drug Use and Drug Subcultures, Feb. 14, 1970, Asilomar, California.

Angrist, B. M., and Gershon, S. 1969. Amphetamine abuse in New York City—1966 to 1968. *Seminars in Psychiatry* 1:195–207.

Calef, V., Gryler, R., Hilles, L., Hofer, R., Kempner, P., Pittel, S. M., and Wallerstein, R. S. 1970. Impairments of ego functions in psychedelic drug users. Paper presented at the Conference on Drug Use and Drug Subcultures Feb. 14, 1970, Asilomar, California.

Carey, J. T., and Mandel, J. 1968. A San Francisco Bay Area "speed scene." *Journal of Health and Social Behavior* 9:164–74.

Connell, P. H. 1958. *Amphetamine psychosis.* London: Oxford University Press.

Ellinwood, E. H., Jr. 1967. Amphetamine psychosis: 1. Description of the individual and process. *Journal of Mental and Nervous Disorders* 144: 273–83.

Frosch, W. A. 1970. The drug abuser's chosen drug. Paper presented at the Conference on Drug Use and Drug Subcultures, Feb. 14, 1970, Asilomar, California.

Hartmann, Dora. 1969. A study of drug-taking adolescents. *The Psychoanalytic Study of the Child* 24:384–98.

Hollister, L. E. 1968. *Chemical psychoses.* Springfield, Ill.: Charles C. Thomas, Publisher.

Kendall, R. F., and Pittel, S. M. 1971. Three portraits of the young drug user: comparison of MMPI group profiles. *Journal of Psychedelic Drugs,* 1971, *3,* 63–66.

Kluver, H. 1966. *Mescal and mechanisms of hallucinations.* Chicago: University of Chicago Press.

Masters, R. E. L., and Houston, I. 1966. *The varieties of psychedelic experience.* New York: Dell Publishing Company, Inc.

Metzner, R., ed. 1968. *The ecstatic adventure.* New York: The Macmillan Company.

Pittel, S. M. 1968. *The current status of the Haight-Ashbury hippie community.* San Francisco: Mount Zion Hospital and Medical Center (mimeo).

———. 1969. Psychological effects of psychedelic drugs: preliminary observations and hypotheses. Paper presented at the Meetings of the Western Psychological Association, May, 1969, Vancouver, B.C., Canada.

Shick, J. F. E., Smith, D. E., and Meyers, F. H. 1969. Use of amphetamines in the Haight-Ashbury subculture. *Journal of Psychedelic Drugs* 2:139–71.

Smith, D. E. 1969. Analysis of variables in high dose methamphetamine dependence. *Journal of Psychedelic Drugs* 2:132–37.

————, Luce, J., and Dernburg, E. A. 1970. The health of Haight-Ashbury. *Transaction* 7:35–45.

Smith, R. C. 1969. The world of the Haight-Ashbury speed freak. *Journal of Psychedelic Drugs* 2:172–88.

von Hoffman, N. 1968. *We are the people our parents warned us against.* Chicago: Quadrangle Books.

Wieder, H., and Kaplan, E. H. 1969. Drug use in adolescents. *The Psychoanyalytic Study of the Child* 24:399–431.

Wiener, A. 1969. *Speed hurts.* San Francisco: Amphetamine Research Project.

cocaine:

champagne of uppers

Nancy A. Eiswirth / David E. Smith, M.D.
/ Donald R. Wesson, M.D.

> If it goes well, I will write an essay on it [cocaine] and I expect
> it will win its place in therapeutics, by the side of morphium and
> superior to it. . . . I take very small doses of it regularly against
> depression and against indigestion, and with the most brilliant
> success. I hope it will be able to abolish the most intractable
> vomiting, even when this is due to severe pain; in short it is only
> now that I feel I am a doctor, since I have helped one patient and
> hope to help more.
>
> *Sigmund Freud*
> *May 7, 1884*

introduction

Sigmund Freud was only one of many notables who praised the
abilities of cocaine. For Freud cocaine held the promise of curing
the most distressing of diseases; for others, such as the fictional Sher-
lock Holmes, cocaine made the dull routine of existence bearable.
The drug, however, has not always enjoyed such distinguished
acclaim and has been damned as much as it has been praised. At
one time sanctified as a gift from the gods and hoarded by kings and
aristocrats, cocaine was later denounced as the "third scourge of
mankind," and still later was shunned by all except inner city
ghetto dwellers and social outcasts.

As America's drug culture moved into the 1970s cocaine was rein-
stated as a popular drug on several socioeconomic levels as is
graphically portrayed in one of 1973s most popular and controver-

sial films, *Superfly*. While recognized medical uses of cocaine are still extremely small, illicit distribution of the drug is booming. Cocaine is now an "in" drug and the demand for it is great. Young thrill-seekers, counterculture youth, and middle-class swingers—as well as drug abusers—are willing to experiment with cocaine and determine for themselves if the cocaine "high" is worthy of its historical reputation.

history

The recorded history of cocaine begins with the ancient Incan civilization of South America. Incan legends describe the harvesting and chewing of the leaves of a shrub now know as *Erythroxylon coca*.[1] An integral part of the Incan religion, the plant was accorded a divine status and controlled by the religious and political leaders of the Incans. Coca leaves were dispensed by the Incan ruler during important religious ceremonies or as a reward for outstanding service. Over the centuries and especially following the advent of the Spanish conquistadors and the resulting destruction of the Incan civilization, use of the coca leaves became more widespread and a part of everyday life for all classes of Indians. Chewing a combination of coca leaves and lime alleviated the fatigue caused by arduous physical labor and made the Indians' daily life more enjoyable. Mine workers and slaves were paid in coca leaves by the European rulers in order to increase productivity. At the present time coca leaves are still chewed extensively by Andean Indians as a social ritual and mild stimulant, much as coffee drinking is enjoyed in the United States. Members of the upper socioeconomic classes in Peru make tea from coca leaves.

It is important to note that coca leaves used as a stimulant reduce appetite. As the food supply in these areas is limited and therefore quite valuable, the chewing of coca leaves is an adaptive survival mechanism. Dr. Richard Schultes, a botanist from Harvard University, spent 13 years in the Amazon with South American natives and regularly chewed coca leaves for a variety of reasons including suppressing appetite and facilitating performance. It is also of import that Dr. Schultes found no evidence of true addiction to or physical

[1] Although *Erythroxylon coca* is the most widespread spelling for this botanical genus, Dr. Norman Farnsworth, Professor of Pharmacognosy at the University of Illinois Medical Center, feels the correct reference should be *Erythroxylum coca*.

dependence on coca leaves during his stay in South America and
that he easily gave up this practice when he returned to the United
States.[2]

It was not until the late sixteenth century that the coca leaves
were introduced to the European continent. Little attention was
aroused by this strange new plant until 1859 when Paolo Mante-
gazzo declared coca leaves to be a great new weapon against disease.
In 1860 Alfred Neimann isolated cocaine from the leaves of the
coca plant. For the next 25 years there still was little interest in the
drug or its properties. Finally in 1884 Sigmund Freud obtained a
sample of the drug and began experimenting with its medical uses.
He declared cocaine to be a wonder drug and published a series
of papers extolling its numerous applications. Freud's papers between 1884 and 1887 repeatedly described his own experimentation
with the drug and his subjective evaluations of cocaine's euphoriant
properties.

According to Freud cocaine could alleviate symptoms of digestive
disorders, asthma, morphine withdrawal, and cachexia, as well as
allay fatigue and act as an aphrodisiac. Cocaine relieved Freud's own
symptoms of depression and chronic fatigue and he enthusiastically
prescribed the drug to friends and patients. One of these was Dr.
Ernst von Fleischl-Marxow, a friend and colleague. It was hoped
that cocaine would relieve Fleischl's addiction to morphine. At first
it seemed that the cocaine treatment was succeeding, but it soon
became necessary to escalate the dosages. This led to chronic intoxication and finally to the development of a full-fledged cocaine psychosis with the patient experiencing such symptoms as "white snakes
creeping over his skin." These signs continued until Fleischl's death
six years later. This experience and the adamant criticism Freud
was receiving from the medical profession soon caused him to abandon both his work with and personal use of cocaine.

Part of Freud's experimentation with cocaine involved an investigation of the drug's anesthetic properties. Both he and a colleague,
Dr. Carl Koller, had worked on the initial experiments but it was
Koller who went on to first successfully use cocaine as a local anesthetic in eye operations in 1884. The interest generated by this discovery soon led other physicians to experiment with the drug and
resulted in its inclusion in a plethora of patent medicines, home
remedies, and beverages. The most famous of these preparations was

[2] Dr. Norman Farnsworth, Professor and Chairman, Department of Pharmacognosy, University of Illinois Medical Center, 1973: personal communication.

a syrup called Coca-Cola. Although Coca-Cola originally contained cocaine, it now utilizes a decocainized extract made from imported coca leaves.

Over the next several years this avid testing and the popularity of cocaine preparations flourished in both Europe and America. However, opposition to and criticism of the drug were also growing. By 1890 the failure of cocaine to produce a cure for opiate or alcohol addiction had become apparent. The medical profession had become aware also of the addicting and psychosis producing nature of cocaine.

No action was taken to control the use of cocaine until 1906 when the United States enacted the Pure Food and Drug Act. The Act required accurate labeling of the contents of all over-the-counter preparations. In 1914 the Harrison Narcotic Tax Act was passed by Congress and cocaine was *legally* classified as a narcotic.[3] The same penalties were imposed for illegal possession of cocaine as for the illegal possession of opium, morphine and heroin. Persons authorized to handle or manufacture cocaine were required to register, pay a fee, and keep records of all narcotics in their possession.

Concurrent with the passage of the Harrison Act cocaine lost much of its popular appeal. The use of cocaine in medicine was for the most part superceded by a new group of synthetic drugs which were safer and more economical to use. The recreational use of cocaine became limited to the underground and by the 1920s cocaine use was restricted almost exclusively to Bohemian jazz cultures and more affluent ghetto dwellers.

During the next 40 years the use of cocaine as an abused drug seemed almost nonexistent. Then in the late 1960s cocaine reemerged as a popular drug among both minority and middle-class white youth. The incidence of cocaine use rose rapidly in 1970 and then increased at a slower rate until mid-1972.

Evidence of the high abuse potential of cocaine has led to its presently being controlled as a Schedule II drug (high abuse potential with small recognized medical use) under the Comprehensive Drug Abuse Prevention and Control Act of 1970. Illegal possession, distribution, or manufacture of cocaine is punishable under federal law as a felony. Cocaine no longer has significant medical uses not easily served by other substances.

According to the recently published Second Report of the National Commission on Marihuana and Drug Abuse much of the

---

[3] The legal classification of cocaine as a narcotic is erroneous. Chemically, cocaine is not an opiate. It is pharmacologically categorized as a stimulant.

cocaine smuggled into the U.S. for illicit use may originate from legitimate production in this country. In 1970, the United States accounted for 88% of the reported world imports of coca leaves. From imported coca leaves the U.S. produced 1033 kilograms of cocaine and exported 725 kilograms. The Commission suggested that some of the cocaine shipped out of the United States was diverted in the receiving countries and smuggled back into this country for illegal distribution.

low dose chronic use

The pattern of chewing coca leaves or using them to make tea by Andean inhabitants involves only small doses of cocaine. Leaves of the coca plant contain only 0.6–1.8% cocaine. Thus the leaf chewers or tea drinkers are ingesting little cocaine; the rest of the coca ingredients are harmless alkaloids. Many individuals are able to use cocaine on a regular basis for months or years and experience no serious adverse effects. Among two million South American Indians who routinely chew cocaine leaves cases of adverse reaction—as seen with high dose use—are experienced only infrequently. Also, outside of stained teeth there seems to be little evidence of physical harm occurring to the Indians.

high dose use patterns in america

At present cocaine is very much available to street drug buyers if they can afford its extravagant price. "Coke," "snow," "gold dust," "bernice," "the rich man's drug" or "the pimp's drug" (all slang terms for cocaine) can be bought on the street for $500 to $1500 an ounce or about $50 a gram. For the user the coke high seems to be well worth its price because of its euphoric and stimulant properties.

The drug can be either snorted or injected. Snorting consists of sharply inhaling cocaine powder through one nostril while closing the other. The material is usually chopped up into a fine powder with a razor blade, arranged into fine lines or columns and then sniffed. Thus a cocaine user may say, "I just snorted two lines of coke," describing the ritual just outlined. Silver straws, expensive coke spoons, or a rolled one hundred dollar bill are often used as symbols of affluence when snorting cocaine.

What the user experiences are 15 to 20 minutes of pleasurable exhilaration and euphoria. These effects appear to be indistinguishable from those caused by the amphetamines. Most users do *claim* one difference though: "Speed kills but coke heightens all your senses." The coke high is unique, combining a charge of energy and exuberance with increased physical and mental capabilities, according to its users. Cocaine is also claimed to be an aphrodisiac. All of these subjective interpretations of this stimulant experience produce an aura that accounts in part for the drug's high price.

Typically, "coke-heads" talk a lot and feel energetic and self-confident until the tensed, "wired" high of cocaine is replaced by nervousness and depression which can last for hours or days. Irritability, loss of temperature sensations and tightening of muscles often accompany cocaine's postreactive depressive state. This depression is in such marked contrast to the previous pleasurable sensations that heavy users will continue to sniff or inject cocaine every ten minutes or so for several hours in order to avoid the onset of depressive symptoms.

A second method of maintaining the euphoria produced by cocaine is to administer it in combination with a longer lasting euphoriant such as heroin. Mixtures of cocaine and heroin are often sold on the street as "speedballs."

Usually the coke-head is a multiple drug user. Between cocaine highs he may use marijuana, amphetamines, barbiturates, tranquilizers, or all of these. Like the "speed freak" the coke-head may also use sedatives and narcotics to combat unpleasant central nervous system (CNS) effects of cocaine, or when he wishes to "come down."

Cocaine is also a popular drug among methadone maintenance clients. Since cocaine will exert its powerful stimulant actions even in the presence of opiates, a heroin addict on methadone maintenance who still wants a high may turn to cocaine.

The properties of the cocaine high are indeed appealing to the thrill seeker but the hazards inherent in chronic high-dose cocaine use make the drug equally unattractive. A frequent side effect of heavy cocaine snorting is damage to the nasal membranes produced by intense vasoconstriction. After only a few months on the drug the cartilage separating the nasal passages may have rotted away. Heavy users are often identified by their frequent infections of the nasal membranes.

Chronic use in the pursuit of maintaining a constant euphoric state increases the severity of cocaine's stimulant effects. After a few days the pleasurable effects give way to an intense anxiety state with gross paranoid features and auditory and visual hallucinations similar to an amphetamine psychosis.

cocaine toxicity

The lethal dose of cocaine is reported to be 1200 mg. after oral ingestion. After application to mucous membranes cocaine can cause death with a dose as low as 30 mg. The difference in these figures is due to the fact that ingested cocaine is rapidly destroyed in the stomach and is therefore much less toxic than injected cocaine. Since tolerance develops rapidly with heavy cocaine use (as it does with the amphetamines) there is also a considerable variation in these doses. Some cocaine abusers have used as much as 10 grams in a series of frequent injections and have survived because of their tolerance. The usual dose taken by illicit users is about 500 mg. a day. Most users are playing a risky game, however, since there is only a 50% margin between the dose of cocaine that will produce a high and the dose that can kill.

Acute cocaine poisoning runs a very rapid course. The individual quickly becomes restless, garrulous, anxious and confused. Pulse rate is increased and respiration becomes irregular. Nausea, vomiting and abdominal pains are frequent. Convulsions may then appear with the patient eventually lapsing into coma and death resulting from respiratory arrest.

Treatment of cocaine toxicity is accomplished on a symptomatic basis. A sedative such as diazepam (Valium) can be administered for the acute anxiety. With a severe overdose hospitalization with respiratory assistance may be necessary. Once cardiopulmonary function is assured the prognosis for the recovery of an overdose victim is greatly increased. Within a few hours recovery may be complete or persisting headache and listlessness may last for a day or two longer. After recovery psychological support is of utmost importance. Hospitalization and treatment with antipsychotic drugs such as the phenothiazine tranquilizers should be used for the rare case of cocaine-stimulant psychosis following prolonged high dose abuse.

Although psychological dependence on cocaine does occur it is questionable whether cocaine produces true physical dependence even though varying degrees of tolerance do develop to high-dose use. If deprived of his drug the coke-head will not undergo a dramatic withdrawal crisis as is seen with heroin addicts but the compulsion to continue cocaine use is strong because of the severe depression accompanying abstinence. For the cocaine user the remedy for his depression is frequently more cocaine.

buyer beware

One of the major dangers of street drug use is the lack of quality control. Expensive drugs are often diluted or substituted with compounds which produce similar effects. This is especially likely to be true during times of increasing consumer demand.

Much of what is sold as cocaine is not cocaine at all but a substitute or mixture of various drugs. Depending on how a pusher chooses to adulterate his goods, the cocaine user can wind up snorting or shooting almost anything. Data from street drug analysis programs show that drugs like heroin, methamphetamine mixed with local anesthetics such as procaine or tetracaine are sold as cocaine. Samples that do contain cocaine frequently have only a small percentage of actual cocaine with the larger portion being another white, powdery substance such as lactose. The chief danger to the user is that he cannot calculate the amount of cocaine he is using nor even be sure of what drug he is taking. There is no Food and Drug Administration or department of quality control for the drug underground.

REFERENCES

Bejerot, Nils. 1970. A comparison of the effects of cocaine and synthetic central stimulants. *British Journal of Addiction* 65:35–37.

Blejer-Prieto, H. 1965. Coca leaf and Cocaine addiction. *Canadian Medical Association Journal* 93:700–704.

Brecher, Edward M., and the editors of *Consumer Reports*. 1972. *Licit and illicit drugs*. Boston: Little, Brown and Company, pp. 267–307.

Buck, A. A., Sasaki, T. T., Hweitt, J., and Macrae, A. A. 1968. Coca chewing and health: an epidemiological study among residents of a Peruvian village. *American Journal of Epidemiology* 88:159–77.

Burroughs, William S. 1959. *Naked lunch*. New York: Grove Press, Inc.

Chambers, Carl D., Taylor, W. J. Russell, and Moffett, Arthur D. 1972. The incidence of cocaine abuse among methadone maintenance patients. *International Journal of the Addictions* 7:427–41.

Hanna, Joel M. 1971. Responses of Quechua indians to coca ingestion during cold exposure. *American Journal of Physical Anthropology* 34:273–78.

Hopkins, Jerry. 1971. Cocaine: a flash in the pan, a pain in the nose. *Rolling Stone*, April 29, 1971.

Jones, Ernest. 1953. *The life and work of Sigmund Freud,* vol. 1. New York: Basic Books, Inc., Publishers, pp. 78–97.

Martin, R. T. 1970. The role of coca in the history, religion and medicine of South American indians. *Economic Botany* 24:422–38.

National Commission on Marihuana and Drug Abuse, Second report. 1973. *Drug use in america: problem in perspective.* Washington, D.C.: U.S. Government Printing Office.

Newsweek. It's the real thing. 1971. September 27, 1971, p. 124.

New York State Narcotic Addiction Control Commission. 1971. *An Assessment of Drug Use in the General Population. Special Report No. 1: Drug Use in New York State.* New York.

Salser, J. K., Jr. 1970. Cubeo acculturation and its social implications. *Economic Botany,* 24:182–86.

Schmeck, Harold M. 1971. Cocaine is re-emerging as a major problem, while marijuana remains popular. *The New York Times,* November 15, 1971.

Student Association for the Study of Hallucinogens. 1972. STASH fact sheet on cocaine. *Grassroots* (Supplement), February 1972.

barbiturate toxicity and the treatment of barbiturate dependence

Donald R. Wesson, M.D. / David E. Smith, M.D.

The short-acting barbiturates are now widely recognized as drugs of abuse. As with the amphetamines, however, delineating what constitutes abuse is complex and the subject of much divergent opinion. We prefer to avoid the semantic swamp of defining abuse, and focus rather upon particular uses of barbiturates which we do not believe are warranted. For example, the use of barbiturates to produce intoxication is injudicious in our opinion. We hasten to emphasize, however, that this is not because we are against the use of any intoxicants.[1] Rather we believe that our society has ready access to other intoxicants which are associated with less medical risk than barbiturates.

Every society has developed rules and sanctions which dictate the use and limits of use of certain intoxicants and prohibit the use of others. The social determinants giving rise to these rules and sanctions are complex, but develop more from tradition, religion, cultural considerations, and the availability of the drug than from medical considerations.

Our culture is now in a transitional phase in which large numbers of individuals are shifting from alcohol to marijuana as their intoxicant of choice. Eventually our rules and sanctions will change as a result of this shift. However, regardless of the intoxicants culturally sanctioned, a percentage of individuals will use them in such a way as to produce medical or psychiatric sequelae, family dis-

---

[1] We sharply distinguish intoxication at home or in private from public, work, or highway intoxication—which we view from a quite different perspective.

ruption, or conflict with others. In addition, within a drug-saturated culture such as ours, each individual has ready access to a variety of intoxicants, culturally sanctioned or not. The intoxicant an individual chooses in such a situation is influenced by such diverse factors as their psychological predisposition, availability and cost of the drug, cultural attitudes about the drug and drug taking, religious values, peer pressure, current fads, street mythology concerning the drug, and the legal consequences of being caught with the drug.

After the current hysteria focusing on specific drugs subsides, we believe a broader social consciousness can develop which will view drug intoxication of all types in a more uniform perspective, and will focus, for example, on the total number of individuals who use intoxicants of all types. The total number of episodes of intoxication occurring during a specific segment of time within a community is a more meaningful index of the extent of community drug involvement than the incidence of use of a particular intoxicant. Drug-use patterns have shifted so rapidly in the past few years, that what incidence data of specific drug use is available is obsolete by the time it is published. It may be discovered that individuals who now use barbiturates as an intoxicant may well shift to alcohol or opiates for intoxication if denied access to barbiturates. It is beyond the scope of this paper to discuss intoxication as a social phenomenon. We would like to focus instead upon the patterns of barbiturate intoxication, their medical consequences, and the treatment of individuals physically dependent upon barbiturates.

barbiturate use for intoxication

Intoxication with barbiturates is similar to that with alcohol, and is usually accompanied by a high-spirited sense of well-being, medically referred to as disinhibition euphoria. As with any drug experience, however, the subjective responses depend upon the psychological makeup of the individual, the conditions under which the drug is taken, and the expectations of the user, in addition to the pharmacological properties of the drug. The exact effect may vary within the same individual from time to time. Uniformly, however, intoxicating doses produce a reduction in the ability to make accurate judgments and a decreased control of voluntary body movements.

Not all barbiturates have the same propensity to produce disinhibition euphoria. In general, the short- to intermediate-acting barbiturates (secobarbital, pentobarbital, and amobarbital) are preferred by individuals who wish to get "high." Other sedative-hypnotic drugs, including alcohol, can also produce disinhibition, given the proper psychological setting and inclination. Table 1 shows our estimates of the propensities of certain sedative-hypnotics to produce disinhibition.

When purchased by prescription, common trade names of barbiturates include Seconal (secobarbital), Nembutal (pentobarbital), and Tuinal (equal amounts of secobarbital and amobarbital). Generic products are also available by prescription, usually for less cost than trade names.

Black market secobarbital is usually sold in small capsules called "reds," "red devils," "red bullets," "red lilies," "Mexican reds," "downers," or "seggys." Pentobarbital is sold under the black market names of "yellows," "yellow jackets," or "nembies." Tuinal has become a highly preferred drug on the street where it is sold under black market names of "double trouble," "rainbows," "reds and blues," "tooies" or "tootsies."

The quality of black market barbiturates varies widely, as was demonstrated by Bryan Finkle (1971). Dr. Finkle, a forensic toxicologist, analyzed 1,000 black market "reds" seized in 22 different cases in a county south of San Francisco. The actual secobarbital content found ranged from 21 to 113 mg. per capsule. He noted that "reds are almost invariably unmarked #4 size red capsules containing varying amounts of secobarbital in an excipient of lactose or stearic acid and occasionally chalk."

patterns of barbiturate intoxication

chronic intoxication:

Individuals involved are generally in the 30- to 50-year-old age group and obtain their supply of barbiturates from physicians rather than from the black market. Most are of middle or upper socioeconomic class and have no identification with the young drug-taking subcultures. Their general pattern of obtaining intoxicating doses of barbiturates is to visit sequentially several physicians with complaints of difficulty sleeping or nervousness. Also, because of their conventional middle-class appearance, pharmacists are more likely to refill their prescriptions without notifying the physician.

These individuals often go unidentified for some time until confusion, decreased ability to work, and episodes of acute intoxication

Table 1: Estimated Ability of Selected Sedative-hypnotics to
Produce Disinhibition Euphoria

Common Generic Name	Common Trade Name	Estimated Ability to Produce Disinhibition Euphoria*
Alcohol	Many brand names	+ + + +
Amobarbital	Amytal	+ + + +
Butabarbital	Butisol	+ +
Chloral Hydrate	Aquachloral Supprettes Felsules Kessodrate Noctec Rectules Somnos	+ +
Chlordiazepoxide HCl	Libritabs Librium	+ +
Diazepam	Valium	+ + +
Flurazepam HCl	Dalmane	+
Glutethimide	Doriden	+ + +
Meprobamate	Equanil Kesso-Bamate Meprospan Meprotabs Miltown SK-Bamate	+ + +
Methaqualone	Optimil Parest Quaalude Somnafac Sopor	+ + + +
Methyprylon	Noludar	+ + +
Pentobarbital	Nembutal	+ + + +
Phenobarbital	Eskabarb Luminal Solfoton Stental	+
Secobarbital	Seco-8 Seconal	+ + + +
Secobarbital and Amobarbital	Tuinal	+ + + +

* Note: Table based on a scale from + = small tendency to produce disinhibition euphoria to + + + + = high tendency, as observed in "street"
abuse patterns.

with slurred speech and staggering gait finally draw attention to their addiction. In these individuals, overdose due to confusion, loss of memory, and repeated doses is a major medical hazard, as are industrial and motor vehicle accidents.

The following history is fairly typical of this pattern of barbiturate use.

A 44-year-old woman was referred by her internist for evaluation and treatment of barbiturate addiction. Four years previously, he had begun prescribing Seconal (secobarbital) for her sleep disturbances, which developed during a period of illness of her husband. At that time, she was functioning well at her job, a junior executive-type position. Gradually she increased the amount of Seconal she was taking for sleep and then began taking it during the day as well. As her intake of pills increased to 20 per day, she developed progressive difficulty concentrating at her job and was eventually placed on medical leave of absence. Her physician was unaware of her addiction until he began receiving calls from various pharmacists from whom she was frequently refilling his prescriptions. By taking different prescriptions to different pharmacies, she had been able to obtain her increased supply. Thus, at no time had she obtained drugs "illegally," and her value orientation was such that she had little patience with "hippies" and "illegal drug abusers." As her own behavior was rationalized, she saw herself as medically ill and undermedicated by her physician. She was unable to assess the extent of her intoxication, however, and frequently stumbled, had slurred speech and complained of poor memory and inability to concentrate.

episodic intoxication:

This pattern is seen most commonly in teenagers and young adults. Sufficient amounts of barbiturates are taken orally to produce a "high" in much the same manner as others use alcohol. The sources of supply for these individuals are the black market, the family medicine cabinet, and occasionally prescriptions. Primary difficulties associated with this pattern of use are accidental overdose, escalating involvement with drugs of many pharmacological varieties, and the same dangers inherent with teenage alcohol intoxication, e.g. incoordination and motor vehicle accidents.

The following vignette, related at a meeting of young teenagers who had come together to discuss drugs, provides a good description of this type of barbiturate use. One of the most verbal members, a 14-year-old boy, explained:

There are certain people around the school who always have "reds" for sale. They usually cost about 25¢ each or five for a dollar. [At the time of writing—July 1972—the street price of "reds" is 50¢ each in the Haight-Ashbury district of San Francisco.] My friends and I take three to five of them before a movie or a party, and things are a lot more fun. I can even go home "stoned" and my parents don't know what's happening because they can't smell anything on my breath. I'm not worried about getting addicted or anything because it's not like heroin, and I only do it once or twice a week.

intravenous barbiturate use:

This pattern is usually seen in young adults who have a strong commitment to the drug-using subculture, many of whom have "graduated" from multiple "pill popping" and, occasionally, heroin use. Barbiturates are injected primarily for the "rush" effect, an intensely pleasurable warm and drowsy feeling, experienced immediately after injection.

This is by far the most hazardous pattern of barbiturate use. The individual rapidly develops a tolerance to the intoxicating qualities of barbiturates and subsequently increases the dose. Tolerance to the fatal dose, however, does not increase as much as tolerance to the intoxicating dose (see figure 1). Therefore, as the individual increases the dose to maintain the same level of intoxication, the margin between the intoxicating dose and the fatal dose becomes smaller. He is thus exposed to a much greater chance of accidental overdose, possible respiratory arrest, and death. Also to be considered are the dangers inherent to needle use:

1. Serum hepatitis is very common.
2. Injection of live bacteria can produce bacterial endocarditis (an infection of the heart valves), pneumonia, tetanus, and infected abscesses.
3. Syphilis and malaria also can be transmitted by shared needle use.
4. Sterile abscesses are caused by barbiturates injected into the tissues surrounding a vein.
5. Damage of hands and fingers may occur if the drug is mistakenly injected into the artery of the arm instead of the vein (Gay 1971).
6. Allergic reactions may occur to adulterants other than the drug.

The intravenous barbiturate users are known as "barb freaks" within the drug-using subculture and occupy a low social status within that culture. They may become so engrossed in their drug use that they neglect basic hygiene and nutrition. These patterns of personal neglect are intensified by the lassitude mediated by the pharmacology of the drug.

A variant of the intravenous barbiturate pattern is the heroin addict who supplements his heroin with barbiturates when the sup-

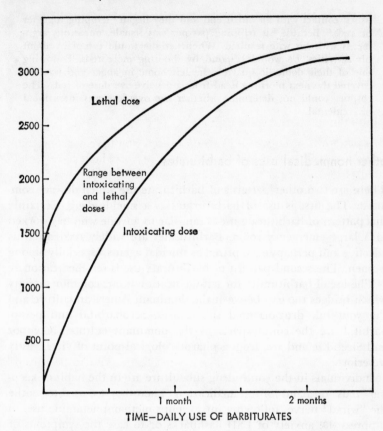

3000 —

Lethal dose

2500 —

2000 —

Range between
intoxicating
and lethal
doses

1500 —

Intoxicating dose

1000 —

500 —

1 month   2 months

TIME—DAILY USE OF BARBITURATES

Time Elapsed Since Daily Use of Barbiturates Initiated

Fig. 1: The relationship between lethal and intoxicating levels of short-acting barbiturates as tolerance develops. Dosages are approximate, due to individual differences in drug tolerance and use patterns.

ply of heroin is low, or unknowingly uses barbiturates because his dealer "cuts" the heroin with it.

The following case history illustrates well, the all too frequent outcome of this type of barbiturate use.

A 35-year-old male was referred for psychiatric treatment following an overdose of barbiturates, which had resulted in a three-day hospitalization. He related an episodic use of intravenous methamphetamine over the past three years. His wife, a nurse, supplied clean syringes and occasionally would also use so that "we could be together." Three months before coming for treatment, he had reestablished contact with an old friend and they began "tripping together on reds." Because his tripping partner was female, numerous arguments with his wife resulted. Whenever she would complain about his activities, he would respond by shooting more reds. Following one of their domestic quarrels, he left home in anger and was discovered the next morning dead from a massive overdose of reds. The coroner could not determine whether the overdose was intentional or accidental.

other nonmedical uses of barbiturates

There are two other patterns of barbiturate use which deserve comment. The first is use of barbiturates as a suicide drug. Certainly this pattern of barbiturate use is familiar to anyone who has worked in a large emergency room. Barbiturates are widely recognized as effective and perhaps even prized as suicidal agents, especially among women. The second pattern of barbiturate use is self-medication.

The use of barbiturates for self-medication is one common activity which bridges the gap between the dominant American culture and the youthful, drug-oriented subcultures. Secobarbital and pentobarbital are the counterparts of the dominant culture's Compoz and Sleep-Eze and are, from a pharmacological point of view, vastly superior.

Individuals in the youth drug subculture are in the habit of keeping "reds" on hand for self-medication. Then they are used to soothe the "wired" nerves following intravenous methamphetamine use, to suppress the anxiety of LSD flashbacks or to ease the symptoms of heroin withdrawal.

With some individuals, the motivation for continuing self-prescribed barbitures seems to be the drug's effectiveness in decreasing clear-cut psychiatric symptoms, such as auditory hallucinations. This type of use could possibly be avoided if the individual had access to acceptable treatment for his psychological difficulties, including a therapist more skilled in the use of psychopharmacy than the patient himself.

addiction and dependency

Barbiturates are capable of producing psychological dependence, physical dependence, and tolerance. Psychological dependence refers to a strong *need* to repeatedly experience the drug effect even in the absence of physical dependence. Physical dependence refers to the establishment of objective signs of withdrawal which occur after the drug is abruptly stopped. Tolerance refers to the adaptation of the body to the drug in such a manner that larger doses are required to produce the original effects. Table 2 compares our estimates of these parameters of commonly used intoxicants.

Table 2: Tolerance and Dependency Effects of Selected Drugs*

Drug	Tolerance	Psychological Dependence	Physical Dependence
Alcohol	+	+ + +	+ + +
Barbiturates	+ +	+ + +	+ + +
Heroin	+ + +	+ + + +	+ + + +
Marijuana	±	+ +	0

* Plus signs indicate (+) small to (+ + + +) high tendency.

treatment of barbiturate dependence

For the individual who has become physically dependent upon barbiturates, abruptly stopping or decreasing the daily amount taken will produce symptoms of barbiturate withdrawal. Unlike withdrawal from narcotics, barbiturate withdrawal in its extreme form consists of convulsions, delirium and hyperplexia and can be life threatening. Inpatient hospitalization should be used during the withdrawal phase of treatment. A previous paper, however, by Gay et al. reported 25 patients who had been withdrawn from barbiturates as outpatients at the Haight-Ashbury Medical Clinic primarily because they refused hospitalization. This outpatient withdrawal was made possible by the use of volunteer outreach workers, friends and volunteers and "street people" who maintained daily contact with the patient. So, while recognizing outpatient withdrawal as a possibility, we nonetheless recommend inpatient hospitalization if at all possible.

The barbiturate withdrawal syndrome in its mild form consists of irritability, restlessness, anxiety and sleep disturbances. Severe withdrawal includes convulsions, psychosis, and death. The severity of the withdrawal symptoms is determined by the regularity and pattern of barbiturate use as well as by marked individual differences. In one study of barbiturate dependence, as little as 600 mg. of secobarbital or pentobarbital taken daily for a month produced withdrawal seizures in some subjects.

Clearly anyone taking more than 1,500 mg. of barbiturates daily for a month or more could be assumed to have a marked physical dependency upon the barbiturates and life threatening sequelae could result if the barbiturates were withdrawn abruptly.

Classically, barbiturate withdrawal is based on a slow reduction of dosage of the addicting agent, usually a short-acting or intermediate-acting barbiturate, at dosages that produce mild toxic signs.

We prefer a method of withdrawal in which phenobarbital is substituted for the short-acting barbiturate in much the same way as methadone is substituted for heroin in narcotic withdrawal. The rationale employed here is that phenobarbital produces smaller fluctuations in barbiturate blood levels because of its longer duration of action. The more constant barbiturate blood level provides added protection against development of withdrawal symptoms and allows for the safe utilization of sub-intoxicating doses during withdrawal. Phenobarbital does not usually produce the disinhibition euphoria or "high" of the short-acting barbiturates. For this reason the patient is more likely to view the phenobarbital as medication rather than as "dope." On occasion this has interesting psychological consequences. Some patients complain that they are unable "to feel anything" from the phenobarbital and become alarmed that they will develop severe withdrawal symptoms. This is observed especially with patients who have tried to withdraw abruptly in the past and experienced marked difficulty.

We find the safety factor for phenobarbital to be far greater than for the short-acting barbiturates. Fatal doses of phenobarbital are several times the toxic dose and the toxic signs such as slurred speech and ataxia produced by phenobarbital are easy to observe.

The dosage of phenobarbital to be given daily is calculated by substituting 30 mg. of phenobarbital for each 100 mg. of the short-acting barbiturate the patient reports using. We allow two days for switching from the short-acting barbiturate to phenobarbital before beginning withdrawal. In spite of the fact that many barbiturate addicts exaggerate or minimize the magnitude of their addiction we find the patient's history to be the best guide in initiating therapy. If the magnitude of the addiction has been grossly overstated toxic symptoms will occur during the first day or so of treatment. Usually this problem is easily managed by omitting one or more doses and recalculating the daily dose.

Should advanced withdrawal symptoms such as tremors, muscular weakness, hyperreflexia or postural hypertension appear at any time during the withdrawal an intramuscular injection of 200 mg. of phenobarbital is given and the daily dose is increased. After stabilization is achieved on the phenobarbital the total daily dose is decreased by 30 mg. per day as long as the withdrawal is proceeding smoothly.

Phenobarbital is metabolized slowly with the half-life of a single dose being 12 to 24 hours. From a pharmacological standpoint, therefore, the total daily dosage could be given in a single daily dose. We prefer a four-times-a-day dosage, however, so the patient can be checked by a nurse for signs of toxicity or withdrawal at least four times a day.

Should toxic symptoms be present one dose or one-fourth of the daily dosage is omitted. We feel that having the dosages divided this way is additional protection against the poor judgment of a single nurse or an inadvertently missed dose of medication.

We would like to emphasize that physical withdrawal from barbiturates is only the first stage of successful rehabilitation of an individual who has based his life style on the use of barbiturates.

barbiturate toxicity and treatment of barbiturate dependency

Most barbiturate-dependent individuals are brought into therapy only by outside legal or social pressure. Unlike the heroin addict— who frequently seeks therapy on his own because he is tired of the daily routine required to raise money for his habit—the barbiturate addict is usually not under financial pressure. A large habit of 2,000 to 3,000 mg. per day could be maintained at a maximum cost of $10 to $15 per day—more typically, $5 to $10 per day.

The combined services of a physician and a vocational rehabilitation counselor and psychological support in the form of individual or (preferably) group therapy are strongly indicated. A long-term (six months to one year) residential treatment center should be considered, especially if the individual has used barbiturates for more than a year or demonstrated suicidal behavior. Unfortunately, "soft drug" residential facilities are rare.

For many barbiturate addicts a completely drug-free existence is not possible unless the individual is in a very supportive environment. The individual's alcohol consumption needs to be closely monitored, since many addicts switch to alcohol to self-medicate anxiety and depressive symptoms or to again experience intoxication.

In our own practice we have seen individuals who found drug-free existence so painful as to contribute to their suicide. At times the individual may need to be treated with long-acting anti-anxiety agents or with anti-depressants. Other individuals can better learn to control their anxiety through hypnosis, meditation or progressive muscle relaxation exercises.

REFERENCES

Finkle, S. Ubiquitous reds: a local perspective on secobarbital abuse. *Clinical Toxicology*, 4:253–264, June, 1971.

Gay, George R. Intra-arterial injection of secobarbital sodium into the brachial artery: sequelae of hand trip. *Anesthesia*, 50:979–981, November, 1971.

Gay, G. R.; Smith, D. E.; Wesson, D. R.; and Sheppard, C. W. A new method of outpatient treatment of barbiturate withdrawal. *Journal of Psychedelic Drugs*, 3(2):81–88, Spring, 1971.

Isbell, H. Treatment of addiction to narcotic drugs. *Medical Clinics of North America*, 34:425–438, 1950.

Shick, J. F. E., et al. Amphetamine toxicity with an analysis of abuse patterns. *Journal of Psychedelic Drugs*, 5(2): Winter, 1972.

Smith, David E., and Wesson, Donald R. Phenobarbital technique for treatment of barbiturate dependence. *Archives of General Psychiatry*, 24:56–60, January, 1971.

Wikler, Abraham. Diagnosis and treatment of drug dependence of the barbiturate type. *American Journal of Psychiatry*, 125:758–765, 1968.

the politics
of barbiturate
and amphetamine abuse

Donald R. Wesson, M.D. / David E.
Smith, M.D. / George R. Gay, M.D.

Most physicians and individuals involved in the dispensing and
control of psychoactive drugs agree that amphetamines and the
"short-acting" barbiturates (secobarbital, pentobarbital, and amobarbital) have a substantial potential for abuse. The definition of
what constitutes abuse however, is the subject of marked differences
in opinion. The term "abuse" has a moral overtone which resurrects
relics of puritanical ethics.

Abuse of drugs available only by prescription is more difficult to
define than abuse of heroin—where use and abuse are usually considered synonymous. While almost everyone would agree that high
dose intravenous amphetamine use or injection of intoxicating doses
of dissolved barbiturates intended for oral use would constitute
abuse of these drugs, there is much disagreement on how to label
the individual who self-medicates himself with commonly used
therapeutic doses of amphetamines or barbiturates, or the individual
who obtains drugs by prescription but who takes more than the
amount prescribed.

Commonly used definitions of abuse of psychoactive drugs reflect
either a sociological or medical perspective. The sociological perspective indicates that drug abuse constitutes the consumption of a
socially unsanctioned drug (the prototype for the most illegal drug
being heroin), or the use of a socially sanctioned drug in a way as
to be a detriment to society or the individual. An example would
be the *overuse* of alcohol to the point where an individual's capacity
to function as a constructive member of his society is grossly im-

paired. Definitions reflecting the medical perspective of psychoactive drug abuse imply situations wherein nonprescribed use of a particular drug exposes the individual to medical or psychological harm. Some definitions use elements of both perspectives. Blum (1970), for example, defines drug abuse as "The regular, excessive use of a drug to the extent that it is damaging to a person's social or vocational adjustment or to his health or is otherwise specifically detrimental to society."

The World Health Organization's Expert Committee on Drug Dependence (1969, p. 6) defines drug abuse in relation to medical practice as "Persistent or sporadic excessive drug use inconsistent with or unrelated to acceptable medical practice."

Discussions of amphetamine and barbiturate abuse frequently fail to draw consistent lines of definition within differing subcultures of society—with strange and sometimes punitive consequences. Because of the social-political implications of being labeled a "drug abuser," this label is more likely to be applied to individuals on the fringes of the dominant culture rather than to those within who may well be demonstrating a similar pattern of drug use.

The drug-taking behavior of members of the dominant culture is more likely to be labeled "misuse" or "overuse." Ultimately the distinction between *abuse, misuse* and *overuse* of medically prescribed drugs is a complex value judgment that one individual or society is making about someone's drug-taking behavior.

In addition to the perspectives of abuse, the individual making the judgment is influenced by such factors as:

1. The social position, age, and occupation of the person taking the drug
2. The quantity of drug taken
3. The purposes for which the drug was taken (i.e., whether to obtain pleasure, to obtain social acceptance, to release tension, to induce sleep, or to commit suicide)
4. The method by which the drug was taken (i.e., by mouth, by injection, or inhaled)
5. The source from which the drug was obtained (i.e., by medical prescription, from friends, or from an illicit peddler or dealer)
6. The degree to which the drug user is "suffering" and the "necessity" for the use of drugs

Parents, teachers, lawyers, physicians, judges, ministers, and others concerned with the issue, may well view drug-using behavior from entirely different viewpoints. In addition to their factual knowledge of drugs and drug use, their judgment will also be influenced by their individual life experiences, personal drug involvement, and beliefs and values concerning:

1. The proper medical use of drugs
2. Good or proper ways of obtaining pleasure or relief from suffering
3. The right of an individual to pursue chemical happiness[1]
4. The role of a *good* government in protecting its subjects from dangerous activities even if it is against their will

Our observations lead us to believe that these many variables are rarely considered at a conscious level when discussing "drug abuse." "Experts" working in the drug abuse field are sometimes the most prone to flagrant subjectivity when identifying drug abuse. There is marked disagreement of "experts" over who is abusing drugs and, specifically, to what extent amphetamine and barbiturate abuse is a problem in our society. In fact, the confusion generated by the term "drug abuse" is so rampant that the concept of abuse has lost precise communicative value.

the prescribing of drugs by physicians

As practicing clinicians, we recognize the importance of allowing individual physicians the option of deviating from "standard" medical practices in unusual cases when the physician has special expertise in the prescribing of psychoactive drugs. This prescribing cannot be completely legislated or dictated by textbooks, or by medical or lay societies. The facts are, however, that most of the psychoactive drug prescribing in this country is done by physicians in general practice or internal medicine (*AMA News* 1972). Many of these physicians had their formal education before the development of the plethora of psychoactive drugs used today. We are especially disturbed by the fact that physicians are constantly bombarded by a barrage of "drug literature"—by mail or through advertising in medical journals—which uses highly sophisticated Madison Avenue techniques. Although this advertising must reflect certain standards established by both the FDA and the medical journal, one cannot ignore the fact that the indications for initiating psychoactive drug therapy are frequently so broad as to include problems of everyday living. Prescribing drugs for these problems is detrimental to the extent that it prevents an individual from learning other methods of coping or exposes the individual to the possibility of adverse

[1] For further comment on the civil rights aspect of drug use, "The Ethics of Addiction," pages 130–139.—ED.

drug reactions of greater consequence than the "condition" treated.

Physicians are *assumed* to be competent to prescribe psychoactive drugs and their therapeutic decisions are *assumed* to be based upon a rational analysis of the drug's indications and side effects. When we reflect, however, upon the fact that many physicians depend upon drug advertising and "detail men" to supply their information concerning the indications for use of psychoactive drugs, we are led to question the informed basis of their decisions.

Fortunately this situation is correctable in several ways. Drug advertising could be stripped of its flashy commercialism to convey only the latest information concerning the drug, including references to sources of additional information comparing it to other drugs that might be alternatively indicated. In addition, medical societies could sponsor seminars and develop educational material for self-study courses, emphasizing the indications, contraindications, and adverse reactions to psychoactive drugs, and education of medical students could better emphasize psychoactive drug prescribing.

Our discussions with students all over the country lead us to believe that this important facet of medical education is usually given only a few hours in pharmacology, usually by instructors who have no actual prescribing experience; or this instruction is relegated to psychiatry in which the students are exposed to severely mentally ill patients whose drug treatment has little relevance to everyday office practice of the nonpsychiatrist.

uses of barbiturates in medicine

> The young physician starts life with twenty drugs for each disease, and the old physician ends life with one drug for twenty diseases.
>
> *Sir William Osler*

Barbiturates have a variety of medical uses of proven value. Although a number of chemically related barbiturates are available, the primary variability which dictates the physician's choice of one over the other is the pharmacological duration of action[2] of that particular barbiturate. A classification of barbiturates based upon this property (Table 1) is useful in describing both the common medical uses and abuses.

---

[2] The pharmacological duration of action is not the same as the rate of metabolism. The short- and ultrashort-acting barbiturates rapidly redistribute themselves into body fat, lowering the level affecting the brain.

Table 1: The Usual Duration of Action of Common Barbiturates

Ultrashort-Acting (1/4 hr. to 3 hrs.)	Short- to Intermediate-Acting (3 to 6 hrs.)	Long-Acting (6 to 24 hrs.)
Thiopental (Penotothal)	Amobarbital (Amytal)	Phenobarbital
Thiamylal (Surital)	Pentobarbital (Nembutal)	
Methohexital (Brevital)	Secobarbital (Seconal)	

Phenobarbital, a long-acting barbiturate, has a well defined and clinically proven use in the control of seizures in epilepsy. It is also commonly employed as a sedative or tranquilizer and is used in the withdrawal of individuals physically dependent upon short-acting barbiturates and other sedative-hypnotics (Smith and Wesson 1970, 1971; Gay et al. 1971). In spite of extensive medical use, phenobarbital is practically never sold on the black market or used to produce a "high" or intoxication.

Thiopental and other ultrashort-acting barbiturates are primarily employed in medical and dental anesthesia, for anesthetic induction, or for short minor surgical procedures. These agents are not "analgesics" (i.e., "pain killers") in the classical sense, but rather ultrashort-acting sedative-hypnotics (or "knock-out" medications). They are not available in oral form, and have not appeared to any extent on the black market.

Secobarbital, pentobarbital, and amobarbital are short- to intermediate-acting barbiturates and are primarily prescribed to treat sleep disturbances. These are the barbiturates most commonly available on the black market, the ones most commonly employed for drug-ingestion suicides, and the ones most likely to be used to produce barbiturate intoxication.

uses of amphetamines in medicine

At the present time, there are few widely accepted clinical uses for the amphetamines. These include:

1. Narcolepsy—a rare disorder in which the individual experiences episodes of a sudden, uncontrollable desire for sleep during sedentary activity. Treatment of this disorder with amphetamines is generally agreed to be of benefit and was the first clinical application of the central nervous system stimulating properties of amphetamines.

2. Hyperkinetic syndrome of childhood (also known as minimal brain damage or MBD)—this disorder is marked by impulsive hyperactive

behavior. The child has difficulty in maintaining attention and is often an underachiever in school in spite of a normal or high IQ. Stimulants (such as the amphetamines or methylphenidate [Ritalin]) have the paradoxical effect of acting as a tranquilizer in this condition. In these cases, stimulants are frequently of benefit in increasing attention span and decreasing hyperactive behavior. This use of amphetamines has recently received widespread public attention and generated considerable professional controversy. Most of this controversy centers around the diagnostic criteria for this disorder and the possible misdiagnosis and overuse of stimulant-type drugs. In some areas of New York and New Jersey, up to 20% of preschool and primary school age children are allegedly given these drugs to control "hyperactivity." This far exceeds any reasonable estimate of the prevalence of this disorder and points out the necessity of leaving the diagnosis and treatment of such protean symptoms as hyperactivity to those with special training and knowledge in this area.

3. Short-term treatment of obesity—while still widely prescribed for the purpose of weight control, the use of amphetamines and related anorexics is controversial. Most of the controversy rages between physicians involved in the treatment of obesity and those physicians involved in the treatment of drug abusers.[3] As an example, William Asher, Executive Director of the American Society of Bariatrics has stated:

There are over 25 million Americans, more than 15% above their standard weight, over 100,000 of whom will die prematurely this year, secondary to obesity and associated conditions. Amphetamines, in spite of all their shortcomings, are the only classes of pharmacological agents which may be of value for use in retraining the eating habits of these obese Americans (Asher 1970).

In opposition, the "drug abuse" orientation to amphetamines is expressed by this quote from John Griffin:

Studies show that these drugs will suppress appetite and that subjects will lose an average of 6.75 pounds more during an 8 to 12 week period than will matched subjects on placebos. At the end of this time, the patient becomes resistant to the effects of the amphetamine and derives little or no further benefit. The cosmetic and health advantages derived from a 6.75 pound weight loss are quite minor. For this reason responsible physicians are of the opinion that amphetamines should not be prescribed for appetite suppression (1969).

The dominant medical opinion appears to be that amphetamines are of short-term benefit in weight reduction for *selected patients* and then only if there is also concomitant alteration in eating habits. Otherwise, any weight loss will be regained as soon as the patient becomes resistant to the anorexic effects of the amphetamines or stops taking them.

---

[3] For further discussion see pages 9–21, "Amphetamine Use and Misuse: A Medico-Legal View"—ED.

4. Mild depression—various stimulants are still advertised for the purpose of alleviating the symptoms of depression. Their use in treating depression, however, is limited by a period of "letdown" when the drug effects cease. This may even intensify or heighten the original depressed mood. Some psychiatrists advocate the short-term use of stimulants during the first weeks of therapy with the tricyclic antidepressants such as imipramine (Tofranil). The rationale in these cases is to override the initial sedative effects of the antidepressant and to give the patient rapid relief of depressed mood until the antidepressant effects of the tricyclic antidepressant becomes evident.

5. Other uses—there are occasionally patients with other disorders which will benefit from the use of amphetamines. This may be the occasional case of Parkinsonism or epilepsy which has not responded to other drugs. Finally, stimulants are occasionally used as an adjunct in psychotherapy.

The decline in the medical use of amphetamines during the past decade has resulted, in part, from the development of newer, more effective drugs and partly from the recognition and widespread concern which has developed about amphetamine abuse.

The medical profession does not recognize as legitimate practice the prescribing of amphetamines to overcome normal fatigue or to increase physical capabilities. The military of many countries have nonetheless sanctioned the use of amphetamines for this purpose. During World War II, amphetamines were used by German Panzer troops. British aviators, as well, used amphetamines to keep awake during long bombing missions and methamphetamine was used extensively by Japanese troops (Leake 1958). Amphetamines were allegedly supplied in our troops' survival kits in Vietnam, presumably for increasing alertness during extended night patrols (*S.F. Chronicle* 1971) and are supplied to astronauts for "emergency use."

some medical-political considerations of drug abuse treatment

From the medical perspective, drugs are used to treat a disease. Given a reasonable probability that a particular drug will benefit or cure a disease process, drugs may be prescribed even though they have a high probability of side effects or severe adverse reactions. It is important to keep in perspective the fact that physicians do not limit accessibility to drugs solely because they may possess a certain potential of danger. Likewise, it would be foolish to restrict the ability of a physician to prescribe a drug purely because it has a potential for "abuse"—*if* at the same time the drug is clinically *necessary* in the treatment of a medical disorder.

Physicians react strongly to individuals who use prescription drugs for recreational purposes. They label such drug use as "deviant," "drug abuse," or "extremely hazardous," focusing on the side effects or adverse reactions. They may recommend institutionalization or compulsory treatment (sometimes punitive in nature) to discourage this "hazardous activity." We find it interesting to compare this response with the estabished "medical role" in regard to other hazardous activities. By way of analogy, skiing, sky diving, mountain climbing, and most active or contact sports have an inherent statistically definable risk of injury or death. The physician's role in relation to injuries caused by participation in these sports is to treat the victim or, in some cases, to act as consultant for primary prevention of injury by recommending particular safety regulations or equipment. Certainly not much enthusiasm could be mobilized among physicians to prohibit football players or skiers from participating in their sports on the grounds that the sport involved has a risk of injury or death.

This discrepancy between the role of physicians in dealing with the medical hazards of nonmedical psychoactive drug use and the hazards of sports or other recreational activities deserves further consideration and study. Perhaps physicians feel more involved because of their knowledge of drugs, or are concerned because they find themselves often accused of having played a role in the increasing use of psychoactive drugs through overprescribing. Could it be that the physician's traditional role as the official prescriber of medications is *threatened* by the individual who uses prescription controlled drugs for recreational purposes?

Some physicians indicate that the amount of risk involved is the most salient feature and that drug taking without prescription for pleasure is more hazardous than participating in other recreational activities. This, of course, depends upon the recreational activity under consideration but does bring into focus the issue of *who* determines the amount of recreationally acceptable risk and *for whom*.

illness or badness

The labeling of a problem determines in great part the nature of the solution devised. Physicians speak the language of illness and thus view drug abuse as either illness itself or a symptom of illness. Without doubt, drug abuse has many medical complications which frequently require medical treatment. However, we question the opinion that the drug-taking behavior *per se* is illness. It appears to us very arbitrary to define taking certain psychoactive drugs as illness, while giving social sanction to others. Do we define the social use of alcohol as illness because of the medical sequelae observed in the chronic alcoholic? Defining drug use as illness may, in fact, focus so narrowly on the problem as to miss the broader political and cultural issues.

We also object to the definition of drug addiction as "mental illness" for political expediency. For example:

> Drug addiction is now considered a mental illness in Indiana as a result of the state's legislature broadening the definition of mental illness to include addiction to alcohol, narcotics, and dangerous drugs. The purpose of the measure was to provide a firm, legal basis for department of mental health special programs of treatment for persons in the categories concerned (*Psychiatric News* 1972).

Our clinical experience confirms that some individuals who take drugs are, indeed, mentally ill, and are using the drugs in an effort to self-medicate and thus to relieve their uncomfortable symptoms (Wellisch 1971). Others have treatable medical illnesses, such as hypoglycemia, vitamin deficiencies, or thyroid disorders, which may have existed prior to and motivated their self-medicating drug use, or which may, in fact, be a *result* of their drug use.

But to define an individual as "mentally ill" because his drug use does not conform with current medical or legislative ideas concerning drug use is a giant step backward.

As an alternative, we would suggest that legislation for barbiturates and amphetamines be established essentially paralleling that for alcohol addiction and intoxication. The Uniform Alcoholism and Intoxication Treatment Act (NCCUSL 1971) would be very appropriate for both barbiturates and amphetamines. This act, which has also been approved by the American Bar Association as of February 7, 1972, contains reasonable guidelines and safeguards for commitments, voluntary treatment, and decriminalization of alcoholism. Within the act, treatment is broadly defined to include a wide range of social, medical, rehabilitive and psychological services.

Political consciousness concerning alcoholism has developed largely independently of that of other drugs owing to our cultural viewpoint that alcohol is not a drug. It is time to begin examining the politics, causes, and social issues of all psychoactive drug taking in a uniform way, and perhaps discover that all are part of the same phenomenon.

Society must have mechanisms for protecting its members against the irresponsible activities of individuals who use drugs in such a way as to present a hazard to other members of society. The highway death toll due to alcohol intoxication and the growing number of auto accidents due to barbiturate intoxication are prime examples which demand action. But is defining an individual as "mentally ill" an appropriate method either for providing treatment or for protecting society? Mental illness has social, political, and medical consequences different from those of drug addiction, and, in fact, psychiatric treatment of the type which is most effective in treating "mental illness" is largely a failure in the treatment of addictions of all types.

The primary motivation for defining drug addiction as mental illness appears to be the currently established distribution of power allowing for involuntary incarceration. At the present, only two social institutions have such power—prisons and mental hospitals. We are therefore locked into a system which dictates that we define the problem as being either criminal or mental illness in order to apply our "solution." We suggest that knowledge in the field of drug addiction is such that neither the criminal model nor the mental illness model alone is appropriate or comprehensive enough.

REFERENCES

AMA News. 1972. Prescribing not factor in drug abuse. April 17, 1972, p. 10.

Asher, William. 1970. Letter to Hon. Thomas F. Eagleton, November 11, 1970. In *Amphetamine legislation, 1971*, pp. 82–83. Washington, D.C.: U.S. Government Printing Office, 1972.

Blum, Richard, and associates. 1970. *Drug 1: society and drugs.* San Francisco: Jossey Bass, Inc.

Gay, George R., Smith, David E., Wesson, Donald R., and Sheppard, Charles. 1971. A new method of outpatient treatment of barbiturate withdrawal. *Journal of Psychedelic Drugs* 3:81–88.

Griffin, John D. 1969. Proposed ban on amphetamine drugs. Paper read November 18, 1969, before the Select Committee on Crime. In *Amphetamine legislation, 1971*, pp. 379–84. Washington, D.C.: U.S. Government Printing Office, 1972.

Leake, Chauncey D. 1958. *The amphetamines.* Springfield, Ill.: Charles C. Thomas, Publisher.

National Conference of Commissioners on Uniform State Laws. 1971. *Uniform Alcoholism and Intoxication Treatment Act.* Drafted at annual conference meeting in its eightieth year, Vail, Colorado. August 21–28, 1971.

Psychiatric News. 1972. Addiction illness. Vol. 8, p. 15.

San Francisco Chronicle. 1971. Ex-GI's say speed is issued. June 24, 1971, p. 12.

Smith, David E. and Wesson, Donald R. 1970. A new method for treatment of barbiturate dependence. *Journal of the American Medical Association* 13:294–95.

————. 1971. Phenobarbital techniques for treatment of barbiturate dependence. *Archives of General Psychiatry* 24:56–60.

Wellisch, D. K., Gay, G. R., Wesson, D. R., and Smith, D. E. 1971. The psychotic heroin addict. *Journal of Psychedelic Drugs* 4:46–49.

World Health Organization. 1969. Sixteenth Report of the Expert Committee on Drug Dependence. Geneva: WHO Technical Report Series, no. 407.

additional related reading

Einstein, Stanley. 1970. *The use and misuse of drugs.* Belmont, California: Wadsworth Publishing Co.

Kalant, Harold, and Kalant, Oriana J. 1971. *Drugs, society and personal choice.* Don Mills, Ontario: General Publishing Co., Ltd.

legitimate and illegitimate distribution of amphetamines and barbiturates

David E. Smith, M.D. / Donald R. Wesson, M.D.

There is a great variety of drugs of abuse in the United States which come from a great variety of sources. Most of this activity is the result of criminal enterprise from start to finish, but a substantial portion of it is based upon what begins as a legitimate endeavor to manufacture drugs for the maintenance or restoration of health. Diversion of these drugs from legitimate purposes, in addition to causing grievous physical and mental harm, is a perversion of honest intentions, changing a benevolent purpose into a particularly hateful one.

> *John E. Ingersoll*
> *Director of the BNDD*
> *July 19, 1972*

At Congressional hearings on amphetamines and barbiturates, much of the focus has been on the vast quantities of legitimately manufactured drugs which reach the street-level black market, and on who is responsible for this diversion. Estimates of the quantities of amphetamines and barbiturates which are so diverted vary greatly with some figures ranging as high as 50%. In prepared testimony presented to the National Commission on Marijuana and Drug Abuse in July of 1972, John Ingersoll, Director of the Bureau of Narcotics and Dangerous Drugs (BNDD), described the magnitude of the problem of trying to monitor the flow of dangerous drugs. The BNDD's files show 457,000 individual active registrants. Included are 471 professional practitioners, and 3,590 miscellaneous categories. Twenty thousand different drug brand names come within the jurisdiction of the BNDD. During the calendar year, 1970, this included

45,000 pounds of amphetamines, and one million pounds of barbiturates. Based on the enforcement experience of the BNDD, diversion exists at virtually every point at which drugs are stored or
distributed. The most common modalities of diversion are as follows:

1. Hijackings and thefts
2. Spurious orders from nonexistent firms
3. Illicit sales by wholesalers, retailers, or practitioners
4. Forged prescriptions
5. Numerous but small-scale diversions from family medicine chests or
   legitimate prescriptions.

Diagram 1 shows our analysis of the legal and illegal distribution
patterns of barbiturates and amphetamines. The patterns are essentially the same for both barbiturates and amphetamines, with this
exception: there is evidence of illegal domestic manufacture of
methamphetamine, whereas there is no evidence of illegal domestic
manufacture of barbiturates at the present time. Points indicated by
an (X) on the diagram are possible sources of diversion. In essence,
any time a shipment of bulk quantities of drugs is made from one
point to another, there is the possibility that part or all of the shipment will be diverted into the black market. Diversion of bulk
shipments accounts for a major portion of the drugs which reach the
black market and requires a well-organized plan to effect such massive diversion.

At the bottom of the diagram are examples of small-scale diversion such as forged prescriptions; burglaries of drug stores, drug
warehouses, and physicians' offices. In addition, there are "pseudo-
patients" who go from physician to physician obtaining prescriptions or samples of barbiturates and amphetamines.

Some barbiturates and amphetamines are manufactured in other
countries and smuggled into the country. The quantities of drugs
which find their way through each particular channel to the black
market are impossible to determine at the present time. There is,
however, ample evidence that all these routes are used to some extent, and an analysis of control measures of one route must take into
consideration the possible consequences on other routes of diversion
and procurement. For example, if the available supplies diverted
from domestic legitimate manufacture are effectively controlled, increasing quantities may reach the black market from foreign sources.

Control alone will not be effective in reducing the demand for
these drugs since drugs of abuse, in general, obey the same rules of

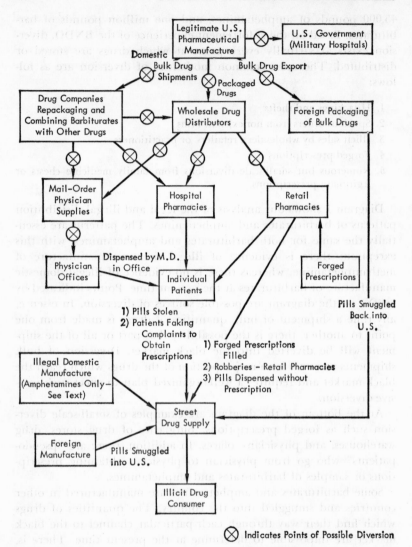

Diagram 1: Routes by which amphetamines and barbiturates reach the black market.

economic supply and demand as any other commodity. A decreased supply in face of a continued demand will increase the price. When the price becomes sufficiently high, industrious entrepreneurs will enter the field and new sources of supplies will be generated. Therefore, any control procedure designed to reduce supply must coincide with an expansion of education and treatment programs to reduce demand for the controlled drugs.

black market versus medical misuse

Much of the testimony presented at recent Congressional hearings by the Pharmaceutical Manufacturers' Association and the American Medical Association has been designed to prove that physicians do not contribute substantially to the black market supply of drugs. Expending energy to whitewash the physician is unfortunate because it avoids delineating the precise roles that the pharmaceutical industry and physicians do play in contributing to the drug problem. A study of diagram 1 will show that diverson of large quantities of drugs to the black market does not involve the physician at all. Yet there are routes which do involve physicians although at the present time this contributes a minor portion of the total amount of drugs available on the black market. A serious error in the analysis of the distribution pattern has been the failure to distinguish between drugs which are distributed through the black market and drugs which are distributed through medical channels to individuals who misuse or overuse the drugs. The physician is the primary contributor through the latter channel.

The distribution of illicitly manufactured drugs via the black market and the distribution via medical channels must be analyzed as separate phenomena despite recent efforts of the pharmaceutical industry to blur this issue. For example, the housewife who is abusing amphetamines is not likely to turn to black market "speed" if her physician stops supplying her medication. Therefore, tighter controls and education of physicians to the abuse potential of amphetamines will be effective in controlling this major portion of amphetamine misuse. These same control measures will not be effective in controlling the portion of black market supply manufactured in underground "speed labs."

funneling of control resources

The BNDD, the Bureau of Customs, and the FDA have a limited amount of funds and resources available for research and field control. Faced with such limited resources, research and control efforts should be focused upon those drugs which have the greatest risk to the individual and society. It follows, therefore, that it would be better to direct the resources of the BNDD and other control agencies toward the control of amphetamines, barbiturates, and heroin trafficking, rather than to dilute them over the entire spectrum of psychotropic drugs. Government agencies have an unfortunate tendency to define a problem in terms of either the amount of drug consumed or the number of individuals involved with the drug. Because of this perspective, marijuana has caught much of the attention and resources of control agencies. Based on the risk to the individual and society, however, the risks of marijuana are minimal compared with the risks associated with the abuse of amphetamines and barbiturates. Control of these substances is, therefore, considerably more urgent and should demand higher priority.

production quotas

Production quotas for the amphetamines were established in the U.S. in 1970. Critics of production control have expressed doubts that decreasing legitimate supply would significantly decrease abuse, pointing to the continued abuse of heroin in spite of *no* legal production. Senator Thomas Eagleton, in his drive to have amphetamines moved from Schedule III to Schedule II of the Controlled Substances Act responded to this criticism as follows:

> Certainly it is true that curbing production of the illicit drug manufacturers will not solve the problem of clandestine laboratories and manufacturing. But surely we cannot sanction diversion of legally produced drugs as a means of discouraging illegal production. We have to meet this problem on both fronts—diversion of legally produced drugs and illegal production (1971).

We believe this puts the diversion into proper perspective. The issue is not simply one of economics but rather of the *ethical responsibilities* of the drug manufacturers. It is ethically irresponsible for legitimate manufacturers of drugs to continue producing quantities as large as the market will bear while realizing that a significant portion of their manufactured drugs is actually finding its way to the black market.

Representatives of the Pharmaceutical Manufacturers' Association however, clearly indicated in their testimony (1971) that production limitations were *not* a responsibility of the manufacturer:

> It has been alleged that the legal production volume of amphetamines represents *over* production, even when the conditions for which such medication is useful therapy are taken into consideration. The role of the manufacturer, of course, is not to make determinations as to whether or not a physician is exercising good medical judgment in his practice. We would not presume to criticize his professional judgment on when and what he should prescribe for a specific patient on a specific occasion. The role of the full-service manufacturer of pharmaceuticals is to insure that the dosage form of the specific medication is available. Our advertisements are limited by federal regulations to specifying only those uses for which the advertised medication has been approved by the Food and Drug Administration. Whether the physician prescribes it for those approved uses, or others, is not subject to review or question by the manufacturers.

These divergent viewpoints can be resolved when the problem is reformulated as how to supply a sufficient quantity of the drugs needed for the practice of high-quality medicine without substantially contributing to the black market supply.

alternatives to control

While successful control of the legitimate distribution of amphetamines and barbiturates is technically possible, this cannot be achieved without utilization of considerable resources. Controls will, of course, require financial support, which will be reflected in increases either in the cost of prescriptions for these agents or in additional governmental funding. Rather than rushing headlong into increasing controls, this may be an appropriate time to consider whether or not the complete elimination of these products from the medical formulary would adversely affect medical practice. During the past ten years, a plethora of new sedative-hypnotics has been developed and marketed. While these agents are all of greater cost than short-acting barbiturates, their inflated cost reflects primarily the drugs' brand-name status. Some of these compounds, particularly the benzodiazepine derivatives, are considerably safer than the barbiturates because their therapeutic/lethal ratio is much greater. A

key to diagram 2

A. Export quotas made consistent with "medical needs" in country being supplied, and assurances that receiving country's government or other appropriate drug-control agency will account for shipments and monitor repackaging and export.

B. Accountability records matched at shipping and receiving points by independent agency audit.

C. We feel this route of delivery is not generally needed for amphetamines and barbiturates.

D. Positive patient ID required for filling of barbiturate or amphetamine prescriptions.

E. Customs inspection and control.

F. Control by local narcotics agencies of BNDD.

G. Education of physician and retraining of prescribing habits to other more effective drugs with lower abuse potential and to sharpen prescribing skills in treatment of anxiety, sleep disorders, obesity, etc.; and altering of advertising and "detailing" practices to physicians from drug manufacturers. Physicians should encourage patients to deal with "symptoms" in a non-drug manner whenever possible.

H. Hand-written BNDD number as well as signature required on prescriptions.

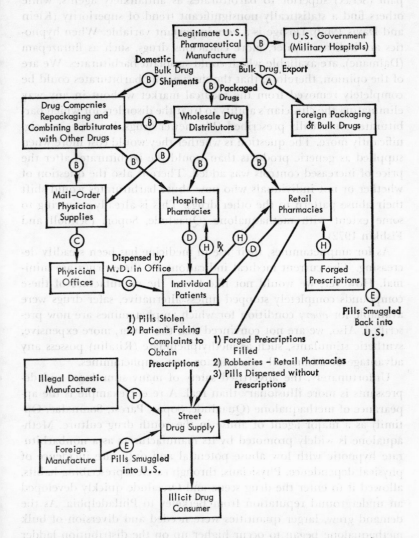

Diagram 2: Amphetamine and barbiturate distribution routes with control point recommendations.

review of the world literature found some studies to indicate drugs such as chlordiazepoxide (Librium), diazepam (Valium), and oxazepam (Serax) superior to barbiturates as antianxiety agents, while others find a statistically nonsignificant trend of superiority (Klein and Davis 1969). Dosage is a very important variable. When hypnotics are indicated, safer, more efficacious drugs, such as flurazepam (Dalmane), are available which could supplant barbiturates. We are of the opinion, therefore, that the short-acting barbiturates could be completely removed from the medical market without in any way eliminating the clinician's ability to treat the disorders for which barbiturates are usually prescribed. The newer drugs, however, cost significantly more. The question is whether they would cost more when supplied as generic products than would the barbiturates after the price of increased controls was added. There is also the question of whether or not individuals who now abuse barbiturates would shift their abuse pattern to the other drugs. This is already occurring to some extent with methaqualone (Quaalude, Sopor) (Schnoll and Fishkin 1972).

As for amphetamines, their use in medicine has been steadily decreasing. The current medical indications for these drugs are minimal. However, we would not like to see the manufacture of these compounds completely stopped unless alternative, safer drugs were available for *every* condition for which amphetamines are now prescribed. Also, we are not convinced that the newer, more expensive, synthetic stimulants, such as methylphenidate (Ritalin) possess any advantage or additional safety factor over amphetamines.

Unfortunately, the advertised safety of many stimulants and depressants is more illusionary than real. A recent example is the appearance of methaqualone (Quaalude, Sopor, Parest, Somnafac, Optimil) as a major agent of abuse in the youth drug culture. Methaqualone is widely promoted by its manufacturers as a nonbarbiturate hypnotic with low abuse potential and only rare incidence of physical dependence. Physicians, through careless prescribing habits, allowed it to enter the drug scene and Quaalude quickly developed an underground reputation from Berkeley to Philadelphia. As the demand grew, larger quantities were needed and diversion of bulk methaqualone began to occur higher up on the distribution ladder (see diagram 2) with the drug being repackaged instead of appearing in its pharmaceutical dosage form. Acute intoxications, overdoses and physical dependence (Schnoll and Fishkin 1972) are now common in many urban areas across the United States and thus a new drug of abuse has been introduced into American society.

conclusion

In summary, the authors feel that it is urgent that the pharmaceutical industry assume much more responsibility in their advertising and distribution of psychoactive drugs. Physicians could certainly be more sophisticated concerning the complexities of drug use and hopefully they can become part of the solution rather than part of the problem. Law enforcement agencies should focus more of their resources on "corporate drug pushers" rather than continually diverting control efforts to highly publicized but peripheral areas of America's drug culture.

REFERENCES

Pharmaceutical Manufacturers' Association. 1971. Statement in *Amphetamine legislation, 1971*, pp. 95–96. Washington, D.C.: U.S. Government Printing Office, 1972.

Eagleton, Thomas F., U.S. Senator. 1971. Correspondence with Dr. W. L. Asher, Executive Director, American Society of Bariatrics. In *Amphetamine legislation, 1971*, p. 84. Washington, D.C.: U.S. Government Printing Office, 1972.

Klein, Donald F., and Davis, John M. 1969. *Diagnosis and drug treatment of psychiatric disorders*, pp. 348–49. Baltimore, Maryland: The Williams and Wilkins Company.

Schnoll, S., and Fishkin, R. Withdrawal syndrome with methaqualone. *Journal of Psychedelic Drugs* 5:79–80. Fall, 1972.

methaqualone:

just another downer

David E. Smith, M.D / Donald R. Wesson, M.D.

introduction

From the East to the West coast there is every indication that methaqualone (available from U.S. drug manufacturers under the brand names of Quaalude, Sopor, Somnafac, Optimil and Parest) is the newest fad in drugs of abuse. Methaqualone was introduced to the American medical market in 1965 for the treatment of insomnia and anxiety. Heavy advertising in medical journals by pharmaceutical manufacturers and promotion by drug salesmen emphasized that methaqualone was a *nonbarbiturate* hypnotic with low abuse potential and only rare incidence of physical dependence. Methaqualone has become widely prescribed by physicians in great part because of their belief that methaqualone is a sedative-hypnotic with none of the abuse potential of short-acting barbiturates. This myth has been fostered by drug company advertising which promotes it as the sedative-hypnotic for those patients who shouldn't take barbiturates.

It was inevitable that methaqualone would be tried by those individuals looking for a "better high" and methaqualone intoxication soon developed a reputation for being especially pleasant. Tributes to the drug spread throughout the country, helped along by publicity in the news media (Zwerdling 1972a) which reported the "alarming" increase in its use nationwide and by articles dubbing the drug "heroin for lovers" (Zwerdling 1972b). The drug even rated the cover of the *Rolling Stone* magazine (Perry 1973).

pharmacological properties

Basically intoxication with methaqualone is similar to intoxication with barbiturates or alcohol and subjects the individual (and those around him) to the same risks: death by overdose, accidents due to confusion and impaired motor coordination, and escalating drug involvement to the point of addiction. Like barbiturate tolerance, tolerance to the intoxicating effects of methaqualone develops more rapidly than does tolerance to the lethal dose. Death has occurred with the ingestion of as little as eight grams in a nontolerant individual. Overdose with methaqualone produces coma, muscle spasm, convulsions, and hemorrhaging due to interference with blood coagulation. Withdrawal from methaqualone dependence is as dangerous as withdrawal from the short-acting barbiturates. The patterns of nonprescribed use of methaqualone are similar to those of oral barbiturates. Methaqualone is sometimes taken in combination with wine, a practice known as "luding out." This is especially hazardous, however, as methaqualone has a compounding effect when taken with alcohol, making the simultaneous use of both drugs particularly likely to result in overdose.

Methaqualone has gained special favor with individuals who are patients in methadone maintenance programs because of the "additive high" the drug combination produces. In addition, street mythology holds that methaqualone is difficult to detect in urine samples containing methadone. This is not the case, however. The myth most likely started when methadone maintenance patients discovered that they could use methaqualone without its being detected in their urine samples. Methaqualone use escaped detection in methadone maintenance programs because it was not one of the drugs routinely looked for in the urine samples required by methadone programs to monitor drug use and not because of any technical difficulties of detection. With the widespread publicity given to the abuse of methaqualone this drug is now being added to the "urine screen" in many methadone programs.

Recently evidence appeared that diversion of pure methaqualone from manufacturers is occurring before it is made into pills or capsules. Sidney Schnoll reported finding two samples of orange capsules sold as "mandrakes" (a street name for the British product, Mandrax, which contains methaqualone and diphenhydramine, an antihistamine) containing over 200 mg. of pure methaqualone hydrochloride without filler (Schnoll and Fishkin 1972). This finding indicates that *bulk* methaqualone is now being diverted from legitimate manufacturing sources.

history of methaqualone abuse in the united states and other countries

With only minimal knowledge of the past history of methaqualone the current pattern of abuse in this country could have been anticipated. Methaqualone was available as an over-the-counter drug in Japan (under the trade name of Hyminal) in 1960 and it began to be widely abused by youth in that country.

During the years 1963 to 1966 a survey of drug addicts in mental hospitals in Japan found 176 out of 411 (42.8%) to be addicted to methaqualone. The primary reason for hospital admission was violent behavior associated with methaqualone abuse. Withdrawal convulsions occurred in 7% of the methaqualone addicts and 9% developed delirium symptoms (Kato 1969).

Nonetheless, when methaqualone was introduced into the American market in 1965 advertising claimed low abuse potential for the drug, and controls over its manufacture, distribution, and prescription were minimal. This negligence might be forgiven as naivete had the same pattern not occurred previously. In 1954 glutethimide (Doriden), and in 1955 ethchlorvynol (Placidyl), were initially acclaimed to be effective nonbarbiturate hypnotics, free from some of the disadvantages of the barbiturates, and without addictive potential. The drugs were widely prescribed but gradually reports of fatal overdoses and addiction appeared in the literature. Controlled clinical studies found the drugs to be comparable to barbiturates in adverse reactions as well as efficacy. Consensus subsequently developed that the drugs were typical central nervous system depressants with no special advantages over the barbiturates.

Whether methaqualone could produce physical dependence was not determined prior to its being marketed in Japan, Germany, England, and the United States. Although physical dependence can be easily studied in laboratory animals, the ability of methaqualone to produce physical dependence was determined primarily by the study of patients who abused the drug.

In a letter to the editor which appeared in the March 12, 1966, *British Medical Journal,* Dr. J. S. Madden of the Addiction Unit of

Moston Hospital, Chester, England, mentioned four individuals who increased their use of methaqualone far beyond the usual prescribed levels. The *Medical Letter,* a bulletin which independently evaluates drugs and therapeutic information for physicians, in citing Dr. Madden in its April 22, 1966, issue indicated that he had reported four cases of physical dependence upon methaqualone. This was erroneous, as Dr. Madden had specifically written: ". . . not having had the opportunity to observe the patients when methaqualone was removed from them, I cannot objectively confirm or deny the presence of an abstinence syndrome."

Gustav J. Martin, Director of Research of William H. Rorer, Inc. (the first pharmaceutical manufacturer to market methaqualone in the U.S.), pointed out the *Medical Letter*'s error in a letter to the editor of the *British Medical Journal* on July 9, 1966. Martin concluded: "This is an unfortunate lapse, and one which, by misinformation, indicts without justification a relatively safe and effective sedative-hypnotic."

The following year Drs. Robin B. Lockhart Ewart and Robin C. Priest, also writing in the *British Medical Journal,* reported a clear case of physical dependence upon methaqualone in a 47-year-old man who was allegedly taking nine grams of methaqualone daily. One evening the man was found unconscious and his supply of methaqualone was taken from him. By the next evening he was ". . . restless and confused, and complained of seeing strangers in the dark corners of the room." The following day he was admitted to a hospital where he was reported to be anxious, restless and having frightening visual hallucinations. He was reported to be in delirium with obvious tremor.

Subsequently other case reports have appeared in both the British and American literature (Schnoll and Fishkin 1972). In 1969 the report of the Japanese experience with methaqualone appeared in the *International Journal of the Addictions* (Kato 1969). Research conducted recently at the Help Free Clinic in Philadelphia and the Haight-Ashbury Free Clinic in San Francisco (Inaba, *et al.* 1973) have documented the high abuse potential and dependency-producing properties of methaqualone as well as its cross-tolerance with the short-acting barbiturates, adequately demonstrating that despite drug company claims methaqualone is "just another downer."

summary and recommendations

In 1973 the Second Report of the National Commission on Marihuana and Drug Abuse concluded: "The risk potential of methaqualone is roughly equivalent to that of the short-acting barbiturates."
Although the Commission did not recommend placing Schedule II
controls over any of the barbiturates it did recommend such controls
for methaqualone:

> Since, unlike the barbiturates, methaqualone does not have large-
> scale medical uses, and does present a significant problem of misuse,
> it should be placed in Schedule II, along with the amphetamines
> (1973).

We feel strongly, however, that *both* methaqualone and the
short-acting barbiturates should be placed in Schedule II because
of their well-demonstrated abuse potential. We feel, further, that
production controls should be placed on "corporate pushers" to reduce the manufacture and diversion of these sedatives. In addition,
the Food and Drug Administration should demand more drug company proof of the lack of abuse potential of other downers to prevent manufacturers from saving millions of dollars by field-testing
their new drugs on American consumers before adequate testing is
performed in animal laboratory situations.

As we have repeatedly stated in this book, measures aimed at reducing *supply* are not enough. Demand-reducing strategies in the
nonopiate area must be improved and should include better physician and consumer education and expanded treatment programs for
those persons destructively involved with sedative-hypnotics and
other nonopiate drugs.

Finally we deplore the growing use of downers like methaqualone
as agents of social control, for in this area questions of involuntary
supply and demand have major constitutional and civil rights rami-
fications. A classic example of our concern in this area was described
in the *San Francisco Bay Guardian*'s article, "San Quentin: Murder
Due to Natural Causes" (Morgan 1973). According to the author of
this article, on February 6, 1973, Tommy Horn, a 23-year-old white
male convict, died of vague natural causes in San Quentin's Adjustment Center. He was given 600 mg. of Quaalude four times a day
(despite the fact that this dose level is several times the manufacturer's recommended dose) because he was a troublesome prisoner.
It is entirely possible that Horn was addicted to Quaalude and

that prison-prescribed misuse of the drug contributed to his death. It appears also that sedative-hypnotics are widely used in such prison environments to keep inmates "quiet and less troublesome" (Morgan 1973).

Recently national leaders, such as New York's Governor Nelson Rockefeller, have placed emphasis on solving America's "drug problem" by putting the illegal drug pusher away for life. We wonder why more attention has not been given to the serious constitutional question raised by the social prescription of legally manufactured drugs like methaqualone for the control of nonmedical, culturally defined symptoms and behavior such as deviance or rebellion against the system.

REFERENCES

Ewart, Robin B. Lockhart, and Priest, Robin G. 1967. Methaqualone addiction and delirium tremens. *British Medical Journal* 3:92–93.

Inaba, D. S., Gay, G. R. Newmeyer, J. A. and Whitehead, Craig. 1973. Methaqualone Abuse. *Journal of the American Medical Association* 224:1505–1509.

Kato, Masaaki. 1969. An epidemiological analysis of the fluctuation of drug dependence in Japan. *International Journal of the Addictions* 4:591–621.

Madden, J. S. 1966. Dependency on methaqualone hydrochloride (Melsedin). *British Medical Journal* 1:676.

Martin, Gustav J. 1966. Dependency on methaqualone hydrochloride (Melsedin). *British Medical Journal* 2:114.

The Medical Letter. 1966. Quaalude and insomnia. Vol. 2, p. 114.

Morgan, Harv. 1973. San Quentin: murder due to natural causes. *San Francisco Bay Guardian,* April 11, 1973, pp. 1–5.

National Commission on Marihuana and Drug Abuse, Second Report. 1973. *Drug use in America: problem in perspective.* Washington, D.C.: U.S. Government Printing Office.

Perry, Charles. 1973. Unconsciousness expansion: the sopor story. *Rolling Stone,* March 29, 1973, pp. 1, 8, 10.

Schnoll, Sidney H., and Fishkin, Ralph. 1972. Withdrawal syndrome with methaqualone. *Journal of Psychedelic Drugs* 5:79–80.

Zwerdling, Daniel. 1972a. Methaqualone: the "safe" drug that isn't very. *Washington Post,* November 12, 1972.

———. 1972b. Methaqualone: hottest drug on the streets. *San Francisco Chronicle,* November 13, 1972.

corporate pushers:

the only thing amusing

about the ethical drug industry

is its name

U.S. Senator Mike Gravel

If tomorrow, by some miracle, every source of illegally grown or manufactured drug were cut off, the U.S. would scarcely feel any withdrawal symptoms, nor would the current drug-abuse epidemic be ended. The sad truth is that our most sophisticated and profitable pushers are the nation's largest pharmaceutical corporations. Somehow, these companies remain almost unnoticed in the intense and well-publicized debate about the causes of the drug epidemic. Each year, the legal drug industry unconcernedly devotes hundreds of millions of dollars to producing a supply of psychotropic drugs— including barbiturates, tranquilizers and amphetamines—in gross excess of any conceivable legitimate medical need. These "mind" drugs are easily available to practically anyone. The same companies go a step further by creating a demand for their products with a slick advertising campaign seemingly designed to persuade every American that it's medically and socially acceptable to shield himself chemically against all the ordinary emotional hazards of life. I see little chance of making significant progress in fighting such propaganda until we recognize these corporate drug pushers as its source and translate that recognition into mass public pressure against them.

We have become numbed to the television commercials that are the most visible example of the companies' crusade to legitimize the casual use of drugs. Day after day, we're told by the country's "electronic hypochondriac," as former FCC Commissioner Thomas Houser labeled television, that drugs are an instant answer to whatever worries, annoys or disturbs us. Dr. Mitchell S. Rosenthal, director of the Phoenix drug-rehabilitation program in New York City, testified at a Senate hearing on the subject that, "While everyone deplores the misuse of psychoactive drugs by young people, a major industry with practically unlimited access to the mass media has been convincing the American people, young and old alike, that drugs effect instant and significant changes, that indeed they work 'miracles' such as making a 'boring woman' exciting to a husband so that he proclaims her 'a new woman.' "

True, the aspirins, Bufferins, Anacins, energizers, blood fortifiers (yes, Geritol *is* a drug) and vitamins you see extolled on the screen dozens of times in an evening don't pose any immediate health hazard to their users. But that's due to their mild strength. In fact, a series of Food and Drug Administration tests has shown that widely used energizers pick you up about as much as does a cup and a half of coffee. At the other end of the spectrum, you can relax just as effectively with any placebo as you can by taking a popular sedative. Even children, who should be watching ads warning of the dangers of drugs, are not spared the constant commercial message on morning kiddie shows that they, too, can pop a pill—a vitamin pill—and feel better fast. Almost unbelievably, three drug companies alone spent $19,000,000 in 1970 urging the kids to get with it. Several recent studies have concluded that children raised by parents who regularly take their medicine in capsules are three to ten times more likely to become drug abusers than are children whose parents don't. What multiple might we expect from children who themselves become accustomed to swallowing the capsules at the age of eight? We might as well allow television advertisements for candy cigarettes on the grounds that candy isn't harmful, and then wonder why our pleas against smoking have so little effect on youngsters.

Besides TV, drug companies use print advertisements in special-interest publications as an especially effective promotional tactic. As much as one billion dollars annually is being spent on a major attack against our resistance to drug use. This effort is aimed exclusively at the nation's 200,000 practicing doctors. In every issue of dozens of medical journals—several of them delivered without subscription charge and paid for entirely by advertising—the pages are laced with ads designed to persuade the physician to prescribe psychotropics for almost every imaginable ailment, anxiety and depression. The idea seems to be that if the doctor's diagnosis does not definitely indicate a specific treatment other than psychotropics, then that *must* be the treatment. Of course, the layman who received one of the 225,000,000 prescriptions for psychotropic drugs last year is almost certainly unaware that this kind of campaign exists. In the absurd history of these ads, doctors have been urged to consider tranquilizers for women who get depressed at the thought of stacks of dishes to wash every night, as antianxiety agents for children afraid of the dark or for military families worried about the father's impending departure. Now, remember that these are dangerous and potentially addictive drugs approved by the Government for treatment of significant mental disorders traceable to pathological causes. In theory, the advertisements must meet FDA standards to this effect, but they generally slip past the Federal obstacle without much difficulty. The fine print at the bottom of the page lists the warnings, side effects and hazards of addiction, which, in the case of the barbiturates, can be more severe than with the opiates. Even assuming the doctors waded through the columns of details, and remembered them, the propaganda would achieve its desired result: making the psychotropics seem an unextraordinary presence. At Senate hearings before a subcommittee of the Small Business Committee chaired by Senator Gaylord Nelson, the Wisconsin Democrat was told that most general practitioners—who prescribe 70 percent of the psychotropics—and even most psychiatrists—who account for another 20 percent—know little or nothing about pharmacology. They are almost as helpless in weighing the scientific basis for the claims made in the ads. And the unbiased, scientific sources of information they do have tend to be financially dependent on the drug companies, as in the case of the medical journals, and are therefore drowned in a sea of specious, misleading Madison Avenue hucksterism. But the ads really speak best for themselves about their philosophy and technique. Here are a couple of examples that illustrate how our corporate drug pushers would have our medical profession view the psychotropics.

In early 1971, two-page spreads began appearing for Serentil, a powerful phenothiazine drug manufactured by Sandoz and approved for use in serious mental disorders, including schizophrenia. Side effects can include drowsiness, dizziness, nausea, vomiting, rash and a host of cardiovascular ailments. (Though no causal relationship had been demonstrated, said the fine print in the ad, "several sudden and unexpected deaths apparently due to cadiac arrest have occurred in patients . . . while taking the drug.") The background for most of the two pages was a plain, green jigsaw puzzle with one piece missing. Looking out from the hole was the face of an an-

guished woman. The bold headline was: "FOR THE ANXIETY THAT
COMES FROM NOT FITTING IN." Below that, the text said that Serentil
was "suggested for *this* type of patient: The newcomer in town who
can't make friends. The organization man who *can't* adjust to altered status within his company. The woman who *can't* get along
with her new daughter-in-law. The executive who *can't* accept re-
tirement." Presumably, by emphasizing the word can't and stating
that a "disordered personality" frequently finds these situations intolerable, Sandoz figured it was protected from charges of exploiting
everyday anxiety situations as new mental illnesses. It was wrong.
The suggestions in this particular ad were too preposterous even
for the normally pliant FDA, which demanded a retraction. Duti -
fully, Sandoz complied, after the damage was done. It had made
claims it knew weren't justified from a medical standpoint. Doctors
read them and then, months later, saw a retraction that admitted a
mistake.

The FDA rarely asks for retractions, generally preferring to let
even some of the most colossal medical nonsense stand unchallenged.
Not a murmur was heard about a series of ads that Aldous Huxley
would surely have included in *Brave New World*—if he'd imagined
them. The three-page ads, for Ritalin, an energizer manufactured by
CIBA, announced to physicians that a brand-new mental illness had
been discovered: "ENVIRONMENTAL DEPRESSION." One installment in
the series dealt with "Noises: A New Social Problem"; another, with
"Tie-Up: The Transportation Problem"; yet another, with "Brown-
out: No Power to the People." In this one, it was explained that
environmental depression may be "often expressed [by the patient]
as listlessness . . . complaints of tiredness." Patients who suffer from
E. D., the doctor was advised, "may not complain specifically of
being depressed. More likely they will complain of tiredness, early-
morning awakening, poor appetite, lethargy, or vague aches and
pains which have no detectable organic basis." What, then, *are* the
specific causes of E. D., as understood by CIBA? "Air conditioners
are turned down, or off. Lights dim. Transportation slows down, or
stops—usually in a long hot summer. This is when comfort, con-
veniences and productivity suffer. So does the emotional outlook of
some individuals. Already frustrated by the constant din around
them, helpless in the face of situations they can't control, and faced
with the daily exposure to bad news and crises, they fall prey to a
phenomenon of the times—one that may overwhelm the patient
and may cause symptoms of mild depression to occur more frequently." By the standard of being mildly depressed from brown-

outs, bad news and crises, is there anyone who *shouldn't* be taking Ritalin? As the ad says, "Ritalin will not help all depressed patients faced with environmental problems, and it certainly won't change those problems or an individual's response to them. But Ritalin can improve outlook . . . help get your patients moving again."

I should say it can. It is addictive if used excessively, and during withdrawal, says the fine print in the ad, "effects of chronic over-activity can be unmasked." Get them moving again!

Women are particularly victimized in, and by, these ads. Dr. Robert Seidenberg, clinical professor of psychiatry at the State University of New York, who has studied the ads' contents extensively, wrote last year: "The drug industry openly acknowledges the enslavement of women, as shown in an ad with a woman behind bars made up of brooms and mops. The caption reads: 'You can't set her free but you can help her feel less anxious.' Another one pictures a woman who, we are told, has an M.A. degree, but who now must be content with the P.T.A. and housework. This, we are advised, contributes to her gynecological complaints, which should be treated with drugs." Valium, a tranquilizer that can impair mental alertness, was the suggested drug in the latter case. Dr. Seidenberg wryly noted that a better recommendation by the doctor would be that she use the prescription money "as a down payment on an electric dishwasher, or a more radical change in life style."

Naturally, there is no place for women's liberation in these advertisements. "Anyone sensitive to the issues raised by the women's liberation movement would be angered by the recommendation that this woman should be *tranquilized* into accepting her life as it is . . . by medication usually prescribed by a male physician," Dr. David Lewis, director of the Medical Outpatient Department at the Beth Israel Hospital in Boston, testified at Nelson's Senate hearings on this subject last summer. "As you can see, once daily living is defined as disease, how logical it is for us to attempt to treat that disease. I do not believe that the public's health is well served by such advertising." James Bicket, president of the Academy of the General Practice of Pharmacy, put it even more bluntly, testifying that this type of drug advertising has become, all by itself, "a major public health problem."

With the public so alarmed by the drug epidemic, why has so little been done to remedy the situation? The FDA, which last year declared itself "thunderstruck" by the number of ads that go "way overboard," has little preventive power. It cannot demand preclearance of the ads, and each retraction ordered requires months of legal fights against batteries of industry lawyers. Until recently, the Federal Trade Commission showed no particular interest in cracking down on the invalidity of many of the scientific claims. But the principal responsibility for the deterioration of the situation rests not with the Government, which should not have to act as censor in the first place. The medical profession itself is supposed to be a protector of the public health, and if it lived up to that responsibility, the present situation would never have developed. The profession, especially its supposed leading organization, the American Medical Association, deserves ethical and moral blame for developing a severe drug-dependence problem of its own. Apparently for no better reason than money, the AMA publishes even the most aggressively exploitive ads, including those that are patently in violation of the association's own stated policy on drug advertising. There has been no major effort undertaken to unite the profession against the pharmaceutical industry, and anyone suggesting to the AMA that doctors should receive their information on drugs solely from unbiased scientific sources is likely to receive the answer that such a step would mean higher subscription rates for the journal.

Sir William Osler, a famed British physician, once said that "the desire to take medicine is perhaps the greatest feature which distinguishes man from animals." The task of the medical profession, he said, "was educating the masses not to take medicine." The AMA seems not to have heard that little piece of wisdom, and perhaps America's physicians need some education on this point. "Physicians have fallen into a rut and lose sight of alternatives to drug use," Dr. Richard Feinbloom, from Harvard Medical School, testified at Nelson's hearings. "The message we receive is very one-sided. Like the public, we are bombarded with ads for drugs and hear no opposing argument. Our journals and meetings, heavily subsidized by drug companies, are devoid of critical debate on the issues of using psychotropics."

Since the pharmaceutical industry and the medical profession have shown no indication of assuring a balanced message, the Government must act, first by placing an FCC ban on the ads for nonprescription drugs on television, just as liquor and cigarette ads are banned. Failing that, the commission should at least require the networks to provide free air time for public-service ads offering scientific evidence and philosophical arguments against the casual use of these drugs; and it should ban all pill ads from children's programs. Perhaps, also, the time has come for legislation authorizing the FDA to screen the advertisements for psychotropics in medical journals.

These are serious Government interventions, but the consequences of doing nothing about the current laissez-faire attitude toward drug pushing are too great to ignore. Unless we recognize the interconnections between this promotion and today's drug problem, we are going to find ourselves with a crisis of unimaginable proportions by the end of the decade.

the ethics of addiction

Thomas S. Szasz, M.D.

The author believes and attempts to demonstrate that "drug abuse" and "drug addiction" are moral rather than medical problems. The basic issue underlying these problems is: In a conflict between the individual and the state, where should the individual's autonomy end and the state's right to intervene begin? The author suggests that genuine commitment to the ethic of personal freedom and responsibility requires that much as we may disapprove of a person's choice of drug, we must regard freedom of self-medication as a fundamental right.

Much of my work during the past 15 years has been devoted to showing that for the most part psychiatric problems are not medical but moral problems (Szasz 1961, 1970a, 1970b). Almost nowhere is this now more obvious than in the case of addiction; yet almost nowhere is the moral perspective now more vehemently rejected and the medical perspective more ardently embraced.

Lest we take for granted that we know what "drug addiction" or "drug abuse" is, let me begin with a definition of it.

Webster's Third New International Dictionary (unabridged) defines addiction as "the compulsory uncontrolled use of habit-forming drugs beyond the period of medical need or under conditions harmful to society." This definition imputes lack of self-control to the addict over his taking or not taking a drug, a dubious proposition

Read at the 124th annual meeting of the American Psychiatric Associatiin, Washington, D.C., May 3–7, 1971. Reprinted from the American Journal of Psychiatry, 128 (1971) 541–546. Copyright 1971 by the American Psychiatric Association.

at best; at the same time, by classifying an act as an addiction according to whether or not it harms society, it offers a moral definition
of an ostensibly medical condition.

Likewise, the currently popular term "drug abuse" places this behavior squarely in the category of ethics, for it is ethics that deals
with the right and wrong uses of man's power and possessions.

Clearly, drug addiction and drug abuse cannot be defined without
specifying the proper and improper uses of certain pharmacologically active agents. The regular administration of morphine by a
physician to a patient dying of cancer is the paradigm of the proper
use of a narcotic, whereas even its occasional self-administration by
a physically healthy person for the purpose of "pharmacological
pleasure" is the paradigm of drug abuse.

I submit that these judgments have nothing whatsoever to do with
medicine, pharmacology, or psychiatry. They are moral judgments.
Indeed, our present views on addiction are astonishingly similar to
some of our former views on sex. Intercourse in marriage with the
aim of procreation was the paradigm of the proper use of one's
sexual organs, whereas intercourse outside of marriage with the
aim of carnal pleasure was the paradigm of their improper use.
Moreover, until recently masturbation—or self-abuse as it was called
—was professionally declared to be, and popularly accepted as, both
the cause and the symptom of a variety of illnesses.

To be sure, it is now virtually impossible to cite a contemporary
American (or foreign) medical authority to support the concept of
self-abuse. Medical opinion now holds that there is simply no such
thing, that whether a person masturbates or not is medically irrelevant, and that engaging in the practice or refraining from it is a
matter of personal morals or life-style. On the other hand, it is now
virtually impossible to cite a contemporary American (or foreign)
medical authority to oppose the concept of drug abuse. Medical
opinion now holds that drug abuse is a major medical, psychiatric,
and public health problem, that drug addiction is a disease similar
to diabetes, requiring prolonged (or life-long) and careful medically
supervised treatment, and that taking or not taking drugs is primarily, if not solely, a matter of medical concern and responsibility.

the bases of our drug laws

Like any social policy, our drug laws may be examined from two
entirely different points of view: technical and moral. Our present

inclination, however, is either to ignore the moral perspective or to mistake the technical for the moral.

An example of our misplaced overreliance on a technical analysis of the so-called drug problems is the professionalized mendacity about the dangerousness of certain types of drugs. Since most of the propaganda against drug abuse seeks to justify certain repressive policies by appeals to the alleged dangerousness of various drugs, the propagandists often must, in order to enlist significant support, falsify the facts about the true pharmacological properties of the drugs they seek to prohibit. They must do so for two reasons: 1) because there are too many substances in daily use that are just as harmful as, if indeed they are not more harmful than, the substances they want to prohibit, and 2) because they realize that dangerousness alone can *never* be a sufficient justification for prohibiting any drug, substance, or artifact. Thus, the more they ignore the moral dimensions of the problem, the more they must escalate their fraudulent claims about the dangers of drugs.

Clearly, the argument that marijuana—or heroin, or methadone, or morphine—is prohibited because it is addictive or dangerous cannot be supported by facts. For one thing, there are many drugs—from insulin to penicillin—that are neither addictive nor dangerous but are nevertheless also prohibited: they can be obtained only through a physician's prescription. For another, there are many things—from dynamite to guns—that are much more dangerous than narcotics (especially to others!), but that are not prohibited.

As everyone knows, it is still possible in the United States to walk into a store and walk out with a shotgun. We enjoy this right not because we do not believe that guns are dangerous, but because we believe even more strongly that civil liberties are precious. (It also so happens that historical precedent favors those who want to preserve this right, not those who want to abolish it.) At the same time it is not possible in the United States to walk into a store and walk out with a bottle of barbiturates, codeine, or other drug. We are deprived of this right (which the citizens of some other countries, such as Lebanon, enjoy) because we have come to value medical paternalism more highly than the right to obtain and use drugs without recourse to medical intermediaries.

In short, our so-called drug abuse problem is an integral part of our present social ethic, which accepts "protections" and repressions justified by appeals to health similar to those that medieval societies accepted when they were justified by appeals to faith. The problem of drug abuse (as we now know it) is one of the inevitable consequences of the medical monopoly over drugs, a monopoly whose value is daily acclaimed by science and law, state and church, the professions and the laity. As formerly the Church regulated man's relations to God, so Medicine now regulates his relations to his body. Deviation from the rules set forth by the Church was then considered heresy and was punished by appropriate theological sanctions, called penance; deviation from the rules set forth by Medicine is now considered drug abuse (or some sort of "mental illness") and is punished by appropriate medical sanctions, called treatment.

The problem of drug abuse will thus be with us so long as we live under medical tutelage. This is not to say that if all access to drugs were free, some people would not medicate themselves in ways that might upset us or harm them. That, of course, is precisely what happened when religious practices became free.

legitimizing social policies

To command adherence, social policy must be respected, and to be respected, it must be considered legitimate. In our society there are two principal sources of legitimacy: tradition and science.

Time is a supreme ethical arbiter. Whatever a social practice might be, if people engage in it, generation after generation, then that practice becomes accepted not only as necessary but also as good. Slavery is an example.

Many opponents of illegal drugs thus admit that tobacco may be more harmful to health than marijuana; nevertheless, they urge that smoking tobacco should be legal but smoking marijuana should not be, because the former habit is socially accepted while the latter is not. This is a perfectly reasonable argument. But let us understand it for what it is: a plea for legitimizing old and accepted practices, and for illegitimizing novel and unaccepted ones. It is a justification that rests on precedence, not on evidence.

The other basis for legitimizing policy, increasingly more important in the modern world, is science. In matters of health—a vast and increasingly elastic category—physicians thus play important roles not only as healers, but also as legitimizers, and as illegitimizers. One result is that, regardless of the pharmacological effects of a drug on the person who takes it, if he obtains it through a physician and uses it under medical supervision, that use is ipso facto legitimate and proper, but if he obtains it through nonmedical channels and uses it without medical supervision (and especially if the drug is illegal and the individual uses it solely for the purpose of altering his mental state), then that use is ipso facto illegitimate and improper. In short, being medicated by a doctor is drug use, while self-medication (especially with certain classes of drugs) is drug abuse.

Again, it is perfectly reasonable to insist on such an arrangement. But let us understand it for what it is: a plea for legitimizing what doctors do, because they do it with "good therapeutic" intent, and for illegitimizing what laymen do, because they do it with bad self-abusive ("masturbatory") intent. This justification rests on the principle of professionalism, not of pharmacology. Hence it is that we applaud the systematic medical use of methadone and call it "treatment for heroin addiction," but decry the occasional nonmedical use of marijuana and call it "dangerous drug abuse."

Our present concept of drug abuse thus articulates and symbolizes a fundamental policy of Scientific Medicine: namely, that a layman should not medicate his own body but should place its medical care under the supervision of a duly accredited physician. Before the Reformation, the practice of True Christianity rested on a similar policy: namely, that a layman should not himself commune with God but should place his spiritual care under the supervision of a duly accredited priest.

The self-interests of the Church and of Medicine in such policies are obvious enough. What might be less obvious is the interest of the laity in them: by delegating responsibility for the spiritual and medical welfare of the people to a class of authoritatively accredited specialists, these policies—and the practices they ensure—relieve individuals from assuming the burdens of these responsibilities for themselves. As I see it then, our present problems with drug use and drug abuse are among the consequences of our pervasive ambivalence about personal autonomy and responsibility.

Luther's chief heresy was to remove the priest as intermediary between man and God, giving the former direct access to the latter. He also demystified the language in which man could henceforth address God, approving for this purpose what until then had significantly been called the "vulgar" tongue. But perhaps it is true that familiarity breeds contempt: Protestantism was not just a new form of Christianity, but the beginning of its end, at least as it had been known until then.

I propose a medical reformation analogous to the Protestant Reformation, specifically a "protest" against the systematic mystification of man's relationship to his body and his professionalized separation from it. The immediate aim of this reform would be to remove the physician as intermediary between man and his body and to give the layman direct access to the language and contents of the pharmacopoeia. It is significant that until recently physicians wrote prescriptions in Latin, and that medical diagnoses and treatments are still couched in a jargon whose chief aim is to awe and mystify the laity. Were man to have unencumbered access to his own body and the means of chemically altering it, it would spell the end of Medicine, at least as we now know it. This is why, with faith in Scientific Medicine so strong, there is little interest in this kind of medical reform: physicians fear the loss of their privileges; laymen, the loss of their protections.

Our present policies with respect to drug use and drug abuse thus constitute a covert plea for legitimizing certain privileges on the part of physicians and for illegitimizing certain practices on the part of everyone else. The upshot is that we act as if we believed that only doctors should be allowed to dispense narcotics, just as we used to believe that only priests should be allowed to dispense absolution.

Fortunately, however, we do not yet live in a technically perfected world. Our technical approach to the "drug problem" has thus led, and will undoubtedly continue to lead, to some curious attempts to combat it.

In one such attempt, the American government is now pressuring Turkey to restrict its farmers from growing poppy (the source of morphine and heroin) (*Time* 1970). If turnabout is fair play, perhaps we should expect the Turkish government to pressure the United States to restrict its farmers from growing corn and wheat. Or should we assume that Muslims have enough self-control to leave alcohol alone, but that Christians need all the controls politicians, policemen, and physicians, both native and foreign, can bring to bear on them to enable them to leave opiates alone?

In another such attempt, the California Civil Liberties Union has recently sued to enforce a paroled heroin addict's "right to methadone maintenance treatment" (1970). In this view, the addict has more rights than the nonaddict: for the former, methadone supplied at taxpayer's expense is a "right"; for the latter, methadone supplied at his own expense is evidence of addiction.

the right of self-medication

I believe that just as we regard freedom of speech and religion as fundamental rights, so should we also regard freedom of self-medication as a fundamental right, and instead of mendaciously opposing or mindlessly promoting illicit drugs, we should, paraphrasing Voltaire, adopt as our position: "I disapprove of what you take, but I will defend to the death your right to take it."

However, like most rights, the right of self-medication should apply only to adults, and it should not be an unqualified right. Since these qualifications are important it is necessary to specify their precise range.

John Stuart Mill said (approximately) that a person's right to swing his arm ends where his neighbor's nose begins. Likewise, the limiting condition with respect to self-medication should be the inflicting of actual (as against symbolic) harm on others.

Our present practices with respect to alcohol embody and reflect this individualistic ethic. We have the right to buy, possess, and consume alcoholic beverages. Regardless of how offensive drunkenness might be to a person, he cannot interfere with another person's right to become inebriated so long as that person drinks in the privacy of his own home or at some other appropriate location, and so long as the drinker conducts himself in an otherwise law-abiding manner. In short, we have a right to be intoxicated—in private. Public intoxication is considered an offense against others and is therefore a violation of the criminal law.

The right to self-medication should be hedged in by similar limits. "Public intoxication," not only with alcohol but with any drug, should be an offense punishable by the criminal law. Furthermore, acts that may injure others—such as driving a car—should, when carried out in a drug-intoxicated state, be punished especially strictly and severely. The habitual use of certain drugs, such as alcohol and opiates, may also harm others indirectly by rendering the subject unmotivated for working and thus unemployed. In a society that supports the unemployed such a person would, as a consequence of his own conduct, place a burden on the shoulders of his working neighbors. How society might best guard itself against this sort of hazard I cannot discuss here. However, it is obvious that prohibiting the use of habit-forming drugs offers no protection against this risk, but only further augments the tax burdens laid upon the productive members of society.

The right to self-medication must thus entail unqualified responsibility for the effects of one's drug-intoxicated behavior on others. Unless we are willing to hold ourselves responsible for our own behavior, and hold others responsible for theirs, the liberty to use drugs (or to engage in other acts) degenerates into a license to hurt others. Herein exactly is the catch: we are exceedingly reluctant to hold people responsible for their misbehavior; this is why we prefer diminishing rights to increasing responsibilities. The former requires only the passing of laws, which can then be more or less freely violated or circumvented, whereas the latter requires prosecuting and punishing offenders, which can be accomplished only by just laws justly enforced. The upshot is that we increasingly substitute tenderhearted tyranny for tough-spirited liberty.

Such then would be the situation of adults, were we to regard the freedom to take drugs as a fundamental right similar to the freedom to read and the freedom to worship. What would be the situation of children? Since many people who are now said to be drug addicts or drug abusers are minors, it is especially important that we think clearly about this aspect of the problem.

children and drugs

I *do not* believe, and I *do not* advocate, that children should have a right to ingest, inject, or otherwise use any drug or substance they want. Children do not have the right to drive, drink, vote, marry, make binding contracts, etc.; they acquire these rights at various ages, coming into their full possession at maturity (usually between the ages of 18 and 21). The right to self-medication should similarly be withheld until maturity.

In this connection, it is well to remember that children lack even such basic freedoms as the opportunity to read what they wish or worship God as they choose, freedoms we consider elementary rights for adult Americans. In these as well as other important respects, children are wholly under the jurisdiction of their parents or guardians. The disastrous fact that many parents fail to exercise proper authority over the conduct of their children does not, in my opinion, justify depriving adults of the right to engage in conduct we deem undesirable for children. This remedy only further aggravates the situation. For if we consider it proper to prohibit the use of narcotics by adults to prevent their abuse by children, then we would also have to consider it proper to prohibit sexual intercourse, driving automobiles, piloting airplanes—indeed virtually everything!—because these activities too are likely to be abused by children.

In short, I suggest that "dangerous" drugs be treated, more or less, as alcohol is treated now. Other drugs should be as freely available as are items on the shelves of grocery stores. Neither the use of nar-

cotics nor their possession nor their sale to adults should be prohibited, but only their sale to minors. Of course, this would result
in the ready availability of all kinds of drugs among minors, though
perhaps their availability would be no greater than it is now, but
these drugs would be more visible and hence more easily subject to
proper controls. This arrangement would place responsibility for the
use of all drugs by children where it belongs: on the parents and
their children. This is where the major responsibility rests for the
use of alcohol. It is a tragic symptom of our refusal to take personal
liberty and responsibility seriously that there appears to be no public desire to assume a similar stance toward other "dangerous" drugs.

Consider what would happen if a child should bring a bottle of
gin to school and get drunk there. Would the school authorities
blame the local liquor stores as pushers? Or would they blame the
parents and the child himself? There is liquor in practically every
home in America and yet children rarely bring liquor to school,
whereas marijuana, Dexedrine, heroin, substances that children do
not find in the home and whose very possession is a criminal offense,
frequently find their way into the school.

Our attitude toward sexual activity provides another model for
our attitude toward drugs. Although we generally discourage children below a certain age from engaging in sexual activities with
others (we no longer "guard" them against masturbation), we do not
prohibit such activities by law. What we do prohibit by law is the
sexual seduction of children by adults. The "pharmacological seduction" of children by adults should be similarly punishable. In other
words, adults who give or sell drugs to children should be regarded
as offenders. Such a specific and limited prohibition—as against the
kinds of generalized prohibitions that we had under the Volstead Act
or have now with respect to countless drugs—would be relatively
easy to enforce. Moreover, it would probably be rarely violated, for
there would be little psychological interest and no economic profit
in doing so. On the other hand, the use of drugs by and among
children (without the direct participation of adults) should be a
matter entirely outside the scope of the criminal law, just as is their
engaging in drinking or sexual activities under like circumstances.

There is, of course, a fatal flaw in my proposal. Its adoption would
remove minors from the ranks of our most cherished victims. We
could no longer spy on them and persecute them in the name of
protecting them from committing drug abuse on themselves. Hence,
we cannot—indeed we shall not—abandon such therapeutic tyran-
nizations and treat children as young persons entitled to dignity

from us and owing responsibility to us, until we are ready to cease psychiatrically oppressing children "in their own best interests."

the fundamental issue

Sooner or later we shall have to confront the basic moral and political issue underlying the problem of addiction (and many other problems, such as sexual activity between consenting adults, pornography, contraception, gambling, and suicide), i.e., in a conflict between the individual and the state, where should the former's autonomy end and the latter's right to intervene begin?

The Declaration of Independence speaks of our inalienable right to "life, liberty, and the pursuit of happiness." How are we to interpret this? By asserting that we ought to be free to smoke tobacco but not marijuana? The Constitution and the Bill of Rights are silent on the subject of drugs, implying that the adult citizen has or ought to have the right to medicate his own body as he sees fit.

The nagging questions remain. As American citizens, do we and should we have the right to take narcotics and other drugs? Further, if we take drugs and conduct ourselves as law-abiding citizens, do we and should we have the right to remain unmolested by the government? Lastly, if we take drugs and break the law, do we and should we have the right to be treated as persons accused of crime, rather than as patients accused of mental illness?

These are fundamental questions that are conspicuous by their absence from contemporary discussions of problems of drug abuse and drug addiction. In this area, as in so many others, we have allowed a moral problem to be disguised as a medical question, and have then engaged in shadow-boxing with metaphoric diseases and medical attempts, ranging from the absurd to the appalling, to combat them.

REFERENCES

Civil Liberties. 1970. CLU says addict has right to use methadone. July 1970, p. 5.

Szasz, T. S. 1961. *The myth of mental illness.* New York: Harper & Row, Publishers.

———. 1970a. *Ideology and insanity.* Garden City, N.Y.: Doubleday Anchor Books.

———. 1970b. *The manufacture of madness.* New York: Harper & Row, Publishers.

Time. 1970. Pursuit of the poppy. September 14, 1970, p. 28.

GLOSSARY OF DRUG TERMS

Street drug terminology is constantly evolving. Some of last year's terms are now obsolete, which is our reason for including this glossary.

This list of terms was compiled by Sunshine, Mary Sue, and Nick, counselors at the Drug Detoxification and After-care Section of the Haight-Ashbury Free Medical Clinic. Their goal was to capture current usages on the West Coast.

A.: Amphetamine

Abscess: Infection caused by injection of impure drugs or barbiturates subcutaneously

A-bomb: Mixture of marijuana and cocaine

Alfalfa: Marijuana

Amphetamine blues: A period of depression or apathy following the use of amphetamines (user term)

Artillery: Equipment used for injecting drugs (term used by police)

Baby: Small habit

Backtrac: Blood which is drawn into a syringe while injecting a drug; also see "jack off"

Bad trip: A panic reaction while under the influence of drugs, karma, or life

Bag: A container of drugs—usually one ounce of marijuana or 1/4 teaspoon of heroin

Bagman: A drug supplier; someone used to transport money or goods

Bang: To inject drugs

Barbeque: *See* HOT SHOT

Barbs: Barbiturates

Beans: *See* BENNIES

Bennies: Benzedrine (amphetamine) tablets

Bent: High from a hallucinogen or narcotic; also, perverted

Bernice: Cocaine

Bhang: A powerful form of cannabis, often in liquid form

Biz: Equipment for injecting drugs; also, anything one has to cope with or deal with; also, selling dope

Blasted: Under the influence of drugs (including alcohol)

Blow: Cocaine

Blow it: Lose your cool

Bluebirds: Amytal sodium capsules

Blue devils: Amytal sodium capsules

Blues: Numorphan; paying your dues

Blue velvet: A combination of paregoric and an antihistamine

Boost: To steal

Boost and shoot: Junkie who supports habit by stealing

Bombido: Injectable amphetamine

Boy: Heroin

Bozo: Absolute asshole; no cool whatsoever; worse than a dildo; a burn artist

Bread: Money

Brown: Mexican heroin which is usually brown in color; also, Third World or Latino person

Bud: Marijuana cluster, not quite a top

Bull: Guard in the penitentiary

Bummer *or* **bum trip:** A bad drug trip or life experience

Bunk: Bad dope of any kind; anything misrepresented

Burn: Amount of residue on piece of foil after testing cocaine; also a bad deal—not getting what you thought you were getting

Burned: To receive phony or badly diluted drugs; to have something ripped off; sometimes refers to being turned in to the police

Burned out: Permanently loose from drugs; no energy left whatsoever for anything

Busted: To be arrested; to blow it in front of friends and have them catch you

Button: Peyote button

Buy: To purchase a drug

Buzz: Feeling at the onset of any high

Candy: Barbiturates or any drug you like

Cannabis: Marijuana

Cap: A capsule of drugs, usually heroin; to put drugs into capsules; also, to hustle someone

Carrying: To be in possession of a drug

Cartwheels: Amphetamine tablets

Cat: Fellow; heroin

Cents: One cent equals one dollar

Charged up: Under the influence of drugs; excited

Chipping: Occasional use of heroin; taking small amounts of drugs on an irregular basis

Chippy: An abuser taking small, irregular amounts

Chiva: Latino term for heroin

Chlorals: Chloral hydrate

Christmas trees: Dexamyl Spansules; a mixture of amphetamine and sodium amobarbital

Chota: Puerto Rican slang for an informer

Chump: Idiot or punk

Cibas: Doriden; a sedative hypnotic with high potential for abuse

Clean: Either not carrying drugs or free of a drug dependency; not under the jurisdiction of the criminal justice system

Clean up: To withdraw from drugs

Coast: To nod while on heroin; to lie back or take it easy—not necessarily while high

Coke: Cocaine

Coke-head: Person dependent upon or who really likes cocaine

Coke time: Ready for a good snort

Cold shake *or* **cold cook:** To prepare drugs for injection—usually pills that are hard to dissolve—without the use of heat

Cold shot: A bad deal; a dirty trick

Cold turkey: Drug withdrawal without medication

Collar: Piece of paper around the end of eyedropper to make the needle fit tighter

Come down: To lose the effects of a drug euphoria; also, emotional depression or disappointment

Connect: To purchase drugs; to meet anyone

Connection: A drug supplier; main-man

Cook: To heat a solution of heroin

Cooker: Usually a bottle top or spoon for heating heroin

Cop: To purchase drugs; also narcs, feds, etc.

Copilots: Dexedrine tablets; amphetamine tablets

Cop-out: To alibi, confess, realize one's mistakes; to make excuses

Cotton: Piece of cotton used to strain a drug before shooting it; sometimes saved for later or for someone else

Cotton fever: Chills and fever resulting from using impure or poor quality cotton; could be septicemia if cotton was contaminated with bacteria

Cracking shorts: Breaking into automobiles

Crank: Methamphetamine

Crap: Highly diluted heroin

Crash: Uncomfortable sensations occurring after amphetamine euphoria wears off

Crib: Apartment where one lives; shooting gallery

Croaker: Doctor who deals with treatment of addicts or who writes unethical prescriptions on continuous basis

Crossroads: Amphetamines

Crutch: A holder (matchbook, tweezers, hairpin)

Crystal: Methamphetamine or speed

Dabble: To take small amounts of drugs on an irregular basis

Deal: To be a drug supplier

Deck: A small packet of narcotics; approximately 35 dollars worth of heroin (east coast term)

Desoxyn: Trade name for methamphetamine tablets

Dexies: Dexedrine tablets

Dildo: Idiot; sometimes a term of affection

Dillies: Dilaudid

Dime: Ten dollars

Dime bag: A ten-dollar purchase of narcotics

Dirty: To be in possession of narcotics; to have used narcotics recently

Dolls: Barbiturates

Dollys: Dolophine; methadone tablets

Doojee: Heroin

Doo-wah-diddy: If you don't know by now, don't mess with it

Dope: Narcotics; whatever you get high on—to pot-heads, it's weed; to smack-heads, it's heroin

Downs: Barbiturates; also a depressed state, sometimes related to absence of drugs; anyone or anything that puts you uptight

Dried out: To be withdrawn or detoxified from a drug

Dripper: *See* DROPPER

Drop: To swallow; also, a place where large quantities of drugs are delivered

Dropped: Arrested

Dropper: Usually a medicine dropper for administering heroin or other drugs into the skin or vein

Dry: No dope available

Duck: Easy person to hustle

Dues: Learning through experience; the price you gotta pay

Dynamite: High potency heroin or sometimes a mixture of heroin and another drug; exceptionally good vibes

Eighth: An eighth of an ounce of heroin (two spoons)

Fall: An injection of narcotics; an arrest or a jail term

Fish: *See* DUCK

Five dollar bag: A packet of heroin sold for five dollars

Fix: An injection of narcotics or heroin; to fix or inject a drug

Flake: Cocaine; also, to pass out on any scene or to go to sleep

Flash: The sudden thrill or high from a drug; sudden remembrance of any incident; to vomit after getting off or being drunk

Flea powder: Poor quality narcotics

Flip out: Irrational behavior as a result of drug usage or as a result of any trauma or heavy trip

Floating: Under the influence of drugs

Flying: To be high on a drug, relating only to positive energy

Footballs: Oval-shaped amphetamine sulfate tablets; any oval-shaped pill

Forwards: Amphetamines

Fours: Codeine pills with a #4 on them

Freak: A person who is dependent on a drug; long hair, "hippie" dope smokers; a sexual nonconformist; a peer

Freak out: A panic reaction to LSD or any life experience

Freeze: Numbness of gums and nasal passages due to cocaine; also, just enough coke to freeze your gums; also, no dope available

Fresh and sweet: Out of jail; new on the drug scene

Ganga: Dried leaves of finest female marijuana plants

Garbage: Highly diluted heroin; generally bunk

Geetis: Money (European term)

Geeze: Shooting a drug

Geezer: A narcotic injection

Get down: Shoot dope or express yourself; get off on your main trip

Girl: Cocaine

Go in: To put your money with someone else's in order to cop

Goods: Narcotics; anything you've ripped off

Goofballs: Barbiturates

Goofing: To be under the influence of a barbiturate or just hanging out

Gow-head: An opium addict

Grass: Marijuana

Greasy junky: An addict who relies on others for getting drugs

Grooving: Becoming high on a drug; having a good time

Guide: An experienced LSD user who supervises others while they are on a trip (rarely used, almost obsolete term)

Gun: A hypodermic needle

Gutter junkies: *See* GREASY JUNKIE

H.: Heroin, pronounced her-ron

Habit: Dependence on a drug or anything

Hang tough: Encouragement to an addict to keep it together

Hang-up: A personal problem, a hassle

Hard drugs: Narcotics; heroin, opium derivatives or cocaine

Hard stuff: Morphine, cocaine or heroin

Hash: Hashish

Hay: Marijuana

Hearts: Amphetamines; Dexamyl

Hemp: Marijuana; also, the police

Her: Cocaine

High: Under the influence of drugs or spiritually inspired; together behind your own trip

Him: Heroin

Hit: To take drugs usually as an injection; to purchase drugs; an arrest; to punch someone or inject someone with a drug; to have someone offed (killed)

Holding: To be carrying drugs

Hooked: To be addicted to a drug

Hopped up: Under the influence of drugs; or excited naturally

Hot: Wanted by the police; also, horny or really looking or feeling good

Hot shot: Overdose of heroin; a deliberately poisoned shot intended to kill someone; battery acid or strychnine; a fatal dosage; barbeque

Hustle: To conjure something out of nothing; a game someone runs on someone else to get what they have

Hype: Narcotic addict

Ice cream habit: A small irregular drug habit

Idiot pills: Barbiturates

J.: Joint; marijuana cigarette

Jacks: Heroin tablets

Jay: Marijuana cigarette

Jive: Bad quality anything; phoniness; bullshit

Job: To inject drugs

Joint: A marijuana cigarette; also, the penitentiary; also, a penis

Jones: A habit

Joydust: Vietnamese heroin

Joypop: To inject heroin; to inject small amounts of drugs irregularly intramuscular or subcutaneously

Junk: Heroin

Junkie: Heroin addict

Kef: Marijuana

Key or Ki: A kilogram of a drug

Kick: To rid oneself of a drug dependency; to be without or give up drugs

Kick back: Relax with no hassles

King Kong: Oil burner habit (over $200 per day)

L.: LSD

Lady snow: Cocaine

Laid back: Feeling good about time, place, and situation

Lame: Dumb or stupid move

Layout: The equipment for injecting drugs

Leapers: Stimulants; amphetamines

Lid: One or 3/4 ounce of marijuana—usually $10 to $35, depending on quality

Lid poppers: Amphetamines

Line: Line of snortable dope; usually cocaine on a shiny surface such as a mirror

Lit up: Under the influence of drugs; slightly drunk

Loaded: Very stoned on anything high

Locoweed: Marijuana; also, jimson weed

Looking: In the market for heroin

Luding out: The use of methaqualone plus wine (or other alcohol containing beverage)

Mainline: To inject drugs directly into a vein; to deal directly with all situations

Make a buy *or* **a meet:** To purchase drugs

Man: The pigs; police

Manicure: High grade marijuana with no weeds or stems

Mellow: Happy; relaxed

Meth: Methamphetamine

Mike: A microgram of LSD

Miss: When a drug accidently misses the vein and goes under the skin because the needle wasn't in the vein; if barbiturates, usually results in an abscess

Mojo: Narcotics; energy

Monkey: A drug habit where physical dependence is present

Mota: Marijuana

Mother: A seller of drugs; anybody heavy (also spelled "mutha")

Mr. Man: Bozo with badge

Mushrooms: Psilocybin mushrooms

Narc: Narcotic agent

Nebbie: Nembutal (pentobarbital) capsule

Needle: Hypodermic needle used for injecting drugs; spike

Needle freak: Someone who enjoys injecting almost anything, who gets a sexual "flash" from the injection

Nemby: Nembutal (pentobarbital)

Nickel: Five dollars; five-year jail sentence

Nod: Drowsy, dreamy state as a result of drug usage

Nod out: To pass into a euphoric state in which the head nods to the chest and is jerked back, only to be repeated

O.: Opium

O.D.: Overdose

Off: Withdrawn from drugs; to kill someone; to have gotten high

On a trip: Under the influence of LSD or other hallucinogens; following a clean plan of action; just hanging out

On the nod: Under the influence of drugs

On the street: Out of jail; also, no place to stay

Oranges: Dexedrine (amphetamine)

Outfit: Equipment used for injecting drugs

Overamp: An overdose of amphetamines

Oz: Ounce

Pad: Apartment or any place to live

Panama red: Marijuana grown in Panama—prerequisite is that tops are red in color

Panic: Shortage of drugs on the illegal market

Paper: A prescription or packet of narcotics; a check; especially if it is forged or bad

Paregoric: Camphorated tincture of opium

Partying: Sharing heroin; also, just getting it on

Penned: Sentenced to a federal penitentiary

Pep pills: Amphetamines

Per.: Prescription

P.G.: Paregoric

Piece: A quantity of drugs, usually one ounce; a gun

Pig: Policeman

Pill-head: Habitual user of barbiturates or amphetamines

Pinks: Seconal or secobarbital capsules cut with Darvon or strychnine

Pinned: Pupils of the eyes contracted from heroin

Pipe: Large vein

Plant: Narcotics placed on someone to promote or set a person up for a bust

Poke: A puff of a marijuana cigarette; a toke

Pop: To inject or take a drug

Poppers: Amyl nitrate

Popping: Injecting drugs under the skin

Pot: Marijuana

Pot-head: Marijuana smoker

Punk: Coward; stupid untrustworthy person

Pure: High quality or undiluted heroin or other drug

Push: To sell drugs

Pusher: One who sells drugs

Quacks: Methaqualone, after the trade name Quaalude

Quarter bag: An ounce of marijuana; 1/4 ounce of cocaine; 1/4 spoon of heroin, worth $10 to $20

Rainbows: Tuinal capsules (equal parts of secobarbital and amobarbital)

Rap: To talk

Rat: To inform the police

R.D.: Seconal capsules

Red-and-blues: Tuinal capsules

Red birds: Seconal capsules

Red devils: Seconal capsules

Reds: Seconal capsules

Reefer: A marijuana cigarette

Reg: Short for regular quality marijuana

Roach: The butt of a marijuana cigarette

Rock: Cocaine in rock form

Rope: Marijuana, usually the male plant, used for making good rolling papers

Scag: Heroin

Scam: To hustle whatever one needs or wants, usually an energy drain

Scene: Being around

Score: To obtain or purchase narcotics or sex

Script: A prescription

Seccy: Seconal capsule

Shine on: To put off or ignore

Shit: Heroin (regardless of quality)

Shoot: To inject

Shooting gallery: A place where narcotic addicts inject drugs

Shoot up: To inject drugs

Sick: To need heroin

Sister: Any female, usually black or chicano; also, cocaine

Skip-pop: Inject drugs subcutaneously

Slammed: In jail; hit "up side the head"

Sleeper: Sleeping pill

Smack: Heroin

Sniff: To sniff drugs—usually heroin or cocaine—through the nose

Snitch: Police informer

Snort: To inhale a drug, usually heroin or cocaine

Sopors: Methaqualone, after the trade name Sopor

Speed: Amphetamines, especially methamphetamine, also now used for PCP

Speedball: An injection that combines a stimulant and a depressant; often cocaine mixed with morphine or heroin

Spike: Needle used for injecting drugs

Splash: Speed; amphetamine; methamphetamine

Split: To break away; exit; leave

Spoon: About a gram of drugs

Spores: Psilocybin spores

Square: A nonaddict or committed devotee of the middle class

Stardust: Cocaine

Stash: A hiding place for drugs; wherever you keep something

Stoned: Under the influence of a drug or drugs; high on life

Straight: One cured of a drug dependence or who does not use drugs; square; also, someone you can trust

Strung out: To be sick as a result of drug usage

Stud: Fellow; junk; gigolo

Stuff: A drug; usually refers to heroin depending on one's orientation culturally and racially

Stumblers: Downers, central nervous system depressants

Sugar: Powdered narcotics

Tab: Tablet (pill)

Take off: To experience the high of a drug; to rip somebody off or kill them

Taste: Little bit; small amount of any drug

Tie off: Apply pressure on a vein so it will stand out and injection of the drug will be easier

Together: In control of oneself or situation; cool

Toke: A puff of a marijuana cigarette

Tracks: Needle scars along a vein from chronic drug injections

Trey bag: Three dollar bag of heroin

Trick: Something done to make money

Trip: Tripping; being high on hallucinogens—particularly LSD; having one's attention captured by anything

Tuies: Tuinal—amobarbital and secobarbital in a red-and-blue capsule

Turkey: A capsule purported to be narcotic but filled with a nonnarcotic substance; also known as burn

Turned off: Withdrawn from drugs; not interested; repelled

Turned on: To be under the influence of a drug; to be aware of what's happening

Unit: Works; paraphernalia for injecting drugs

Up: To be under the influence of a drug, usually an amphetamine; feeling positive

Uppers: Stimulants; amphetamines

Using: The use of drugs

Wake up: First hit of heroin of the day, sometimes saved from the night before

Wallbanger: An individual intoxicated and staggering under the influence of alcohol or other downer

Wasted: Under the influence of drugs; also, tired

Water: Speed

Weed: Marijuana

Weekend habit: A small, irregular drug habit

Whites: Amphetamine sulfate tablets

White stuff: Morphine

Works: Equipment used for injecting drugs

Write: To write prescriptions for dope

Yellow jackets: Nembutal capsules (pentobarbital)

Zonked: To be under the influence of a drug

NOTES ON THE EDITORS AND CONTRIBUTORS

DONALD R. WESSON, M.D. was formerly the Chief Psychiatrist at the Haight-Ashbury Free Medical Clinic, San Francisco, California. He is currently Program Director, West Coast Polydrug Abuse Treatment and Research Project, San Francisco and Clinical Instructor, Department of Psychiatry, University of California Medical Center, San Francisco.

DAVID E. SMITH, M.D., M.S. is Founder and Medical Director of the Haight-Ashbury Free Medical Clinic; Assistant Program Director, West Coast Polydrug Abuse Treatment and Research Project and Assistant Clinical Professor of Toxicology, University of California Medical Center, San Francisco. He is coauthor of the books *Love Needs Care* and *It's So Good, Don't Even Try It Once.*

JOHN C. KRAMER, M.D. is Associate Professor, Department of Psychiatry and Department of Pharmacology, University of California at Irvine.

ROBERT G. PINCO, ESQ. is Assistant General Counsel, Special Action Office for Drug Abuse Prevention, Washington, D.C.

J. FRED E. SHICK, M.D. is a former Research Associate at the Haight-Ashbury Free Medical Clinic, San Francisco. He is presently Youth Services Coordinator, Illinois Drug Abuse Program, Chicago, Illinois and Assistant Professor, Department of Psychiatry, University of Chicago, Chicago.

STEPHEN M. PITTEL, PH.D. is Director, Berkeley Center for Drug Studies, Berkeley, California and Professor, The Wright Institute, Berkeley.

RICARDO HOFER is Research Psychologist, Berkeley Center for Drug Studies, Berkeley.

NANCY A. EISWIRTH is a Research Assistant at the West Coast Polydrug Abuse Treatment and Research Project, San Francisco.

GEORGE R. GAY, M.D. is Director of Clinical Activities, Haight-Ashbury Free Medical Clinic, San Francisco.

MIKE GRAVEL is U.S. Senator from Alaska.

THOMAS S. SZASZ, M.D. is Professor of Psychiatry, State University of New York, Upstate Medical Center, Syracuse, New York.